*Romanticism in Perspective: Texts, Cultures, Histories*

General Editors: **Marilyn Gaull**, Professor of English, Temple University/New York University; **Stephen Prickett**, Regius Professor of English Language and Literature, University of Glasgow

This series aims to offer a fresh assessment of Romanticism by looking at it from a wide variety of perspectives. Both comparative and interdisciplinary, it will bring together cognate themes from architecture, art history, landscape gardening, linguistics, literature, philosophy, politics, science, social and political history and theology to deal with original, contentious or as yet unexplored aspects of Romanticism as a Europe-wide phenomenon.

*Titles include*:

Toby R. Benis
ROMANTICISM ON THE ROAD
The Marginal Gains of Wordsworth's Homeless

Frederick Burwick
THOMAS DE QUINCEY
Knowledge and Power

Richard Cronin (*editor*)
1798: THE YEAR OF THE *LYRICAL BALLADS*

Péter Dávidházi
THE ROMANTIC CULT OF SHAKESPEARE
Literary Reception in Anthropological Perspective

Charles Donelan
ROMANTICISM AND MALE FANTASY IN BYRON'S *DON JUAN*
A Marketable Vice

Tim Fulford
ROMANTICISM AND MASCULINITY
Gender, Politics and Poetics in the Writings of Burke, Coleridge, Cobbett, Wordsworth, De Quincey and Hazlitt

Michael J. Hofstetter
THE ROMANTIC IDEA OF A UNIVERSITY
England and Germany, 1770–1850

David Jasper
THE SACRED AND SECULAR CANON IN ROMANTICISM
Preserving the Sacred Truths

Malcolm Kelsall
JEFFERSON AND THE ICONOGRAPHY OF ROMANTICISM
Folk, Land, Culture and the Romantic Nation

Mark S. Lussier
ROMANTIC DYNAMICS
The Poetics of Physicality

Andrew McCann
CULTURAL POLITICS IN THE 1790s
Literature, Radicalism and the Public Sphere

Ayumi Mizukoshi
KEATS, HUNT AND THE AESTHETICS OF PLEASURE

Ashton Nichols
THE REVOLUTIONARY 'I'
Wordsworth and the Politics of Self-Presentation

Jeffrey C. Robinson
RECEPTION AND POETICS IN KEATS
'My Ended Poet'

Anya Taylor
BACCHUS IN ROMANTIC ENGLAND
Writers and Drink, 1780–1830

Nicola Trott and Seamus Perry (*editors*)
1800: THE NEW *LYRICAL BALLADS*

Michael Wiley
ROMANTIC GEOGRAPHY
Wordsworth and Anglo-European Spaces

Eric Wilson
EMERSON'S SUBLIME SCIENCE

John Wyatt
WORDSWORTH'S POEMS OF TRAVEL, 1819–42
'Such Sweet Wayfaring'

**Romanticism in Perspective**
**Series Standing Order ISBN 0–333–71490–3**
(*outside North America only*)

You can receive future titles in this series as they are published by placing a standing order.
Please contact your bookseller or, in case of difficulty, write to us at the address below with
your name and address, the title of the series and the ISBN quoted above.

Customer Services Department, Macmillan Distribution Ltd, Houndmills, Basingstoke,
Hampshire RG21 6XS, England

# The Romantic Idea of a University

## England and Germany, 1770–1850

Michael J. Hofstetter
*Associate Professor of History*
*Southwest State University*
*Marshall*
*Minnesota*

First published 2001 by
PALGRAVE
Houndmills, Basingstoke, Hampshire RG21 6XS and
175 Fifth Avenue, New York, N. Y. 10010
Companies and representatives throughout the world

PALGRAVE is the new global academic imprint of
St. Martin's Press LLC Scholarly and Reference Division and
Palgrave Publishers Ltd (formerly Macmillan Press Ltd).

ISBN 0–333–71888–7

This book is printed on paper suitable for recycling and made from fully managed and sustained forest sources.

A catalogue record for this book is available from the British Library.

Library of Congress Cataloging-in-Publication Data
Hofstetter, Michael J., 1959–
    The romantic idea of a university : England and Germany,
    1770–1850 / Michael J. Hofstetter.
        p. cm. — (Romanticism in perspective)
    Includes bibliographical references and index.
    ISBN 0–333–71888–7
        1. Universities and colleges—England—History—18th century.
    2. Universities and colleges—England—History—19th century. 3.
    Universities and colleges—Germany—History—18th century. 4.
    Universities and colleges—Germany—History—19th century. 5.
    England—Intellectual life—18th century. 6. England—Intellectual
    life—19th century. 7. Germany—Intellectual life—18th century. 8.
    Germany—Intellectual life—19th century. 9. Comparative education.
    I. Title. II. Series.

    LA636.5 .H64 2000
    378.42—dc21
                                                            00–066868

10    9    8    7    6    5    4    3    2    1
10    09    08    07    06    05    04    03    02    01

Printed in Great Britain by Antony Rowe Ltd, Chippenham, Wiltshire

*To Catherine, Campbell and Olivia*

# Contents

# Acknowledgements

I wish to give my sincere thanks to all those who helped make this book possible. I thank the History Department at Northwestern University, Evanston, Illinois, and in particular Professors T. W. Heyck, E. William Monter, Sarah Maza and Lacey Baldwin Smith for their useful comments and criticisms. The University of Minnesota Library and the library at Cambridge University were great resources and were kind enough to grant me privileges as a visiting scholar. I must also thank the Master and Fellows of Trinity College, Cambridge for graciously allowing me access to the Whewell manuscript collection and for granting permission to quote from it. Special thanks go to the Historical Institute at the Friedrich Schiller Universität in Jena, Germany, and to Dr. Professor .Georg Schmidt and Dr. Joachim Bauer for their assistance. I owe a debt to the archives at this university, and to Dr. L. Arnold, chief archivist, and her staff, Frau Seifert, Frau Ritze and Frau Hartleb. Marilyn Gaull and Stephen Prickett, the series editors, have been most supportive. Thanks also go to Bethany College in Lindsborg, Kansas for its support of my efforts while I taught there, and to Southwest State University in Minnesota. Lastly, I acknowledge the great support of my wife Catherine, whose patience, hard work and thoughtful suggestions were crucial for this book. She and my two children, Campbell and Olivia, kept me going through the challenging process of seeing this book to print.

I am, of course, alone responsible for any shortcomings in this work.

# Preface

A visit to a German university in about 1770 would have been physically exciting, but not intellectually so. Duelling fraternities and student riots gave some colour to institutions which were otherwise the lifeless homes of antiquated curricula and an uninterested, mediocre professorate. Oxford and Cambridge were scarcely more stimulating to the mind, peopled as they were with indifferent though less violent students, somnambulant dons, and celibate fellows who drank and hunted to pass their time. The old Idea of a university, based on religious confessions, had ceased to function in Protestant Europe, and no new Idea had arisen to replace it. The Enlightenment, a product of *salon* culture, had largely passed the universities by. But in the ensuing decades, the tranquillity of all Europe would be shattered by the French revolution. Universities would likewise be changed forever – in part, by the intellectual movement which historians choose to call Romanticism, and to the new Idea of a university which arose from it.

This book concerns the romantic Idea of a university. The word 'Idea' takes on a particular meaning in the thought of the late eighteenth century and in this sense is best defined by Immanuel Kant:

> An Idea is nothing other than a concept of perfection which is not yet found in experience.[1]

An Idea does not exist in the physical world; it exists in the mind of man. None the less it may have a key role in history, for it shapes human events by the action it inspires. An Idea manifests itself in human action; although it never finds a fitting home in this world of imperfect mortals, its drives them onward and leaves behind a trail of human, historical experience.

Sheldon Rothblatt, a leading student of Oxbridge in the eighteenth and nineteenth centuries, has argued that Romanticism marked not only the origins of a new Idea of a university, but the birth of the notion that universities even *had* an idea at all.[2] When discussing English thinkers on universities from Coleridge to Newman, Rothblatt notes that 'what is truly lasting about their efforts is not a particular idea of a university, but the idea of an idea of a university.'³ Universities, then, do not have Ideas at all (neither do other things); however, the Romantics, says Rothblatt, made it fashionable to suppose that they did. The present author, however, is too much a child of the Platonic and idealist traditions to be willing to discard Ideas altogether. He accepts the notion that things have purpose and notes that people, even in our sceptical age, are forever seeking that purpose. Even Professor Rothblatt concedes the latter point, noting that the belief that universities have an Idea is 'seductive'.⁴ The term 'Idea' is construed in this work as referring to something that really exists in the mind and that as such has a discernible existence in human history.

Other terms such as 'romantic', 'baroque', 'gothic' and, above all, 'classical' usually have more meaning for scholars reviewing a period than for its long-dead occupants. Some cultural historians object to using the term 'romantic' at all. Other scholars use it in a very closely defined fashion. They would, for example, call the Schlegels, Novalis, Coleridge and Byron Romantics, but argue that Schiller, Goethe, Schelling and Carlyle were not. This book however will employ a broad, synthetic conception of the term. I agree fully with Otto Bollnow, who wrote more than thirty years ago that:

> 'Romanticism', 'Idealism', etc. are generally only belated terms which make historical reality clear to us, but which at no point exist in a 'pure' form. In reality we have only a uniform movement whose supporters, despite differences in age and direction, are bound together by many threads. [In this movement] the true power of an individual thinker appears not in formal consistency, but in a creative union of various ideas.⁵

Some people discussed in this book, such as Kant and Fichte, are generally not considered to be Romantics. But their thoughts about human knowledge, aesthetics and society contributed to the romantic Idea of a university. The term 'Romantic' may be a bit artificial. None the less it seems the only adequate one for the collection of thoughts discussed here.

Scholars have long noted common threads about nature, the imagination and the divine which transcend national boundaries in the Romantic Movement. René Wellek clearly delineates some of these as they appear in poetry, including Romanticism's stress on the imagination and its use of symbols. Poetry, of course, does not exist in isolation – indeed, in the Romantic Age, nothing did. Whatever else may be said about Romanticism, one must agree that it was more than a few isolated ideas or theories, but an all-encompassing *Weltanschauung* which comprised art, politics, religion and higher education.

Bollnow also argues that a specifically romantic approach to primary education appeared between 1800 and 1830. It was closely tied to the aesthetics, social theory and psychology of the Romantics; so, too, was the romantic Idea of a university. At the foundation was the romantic view of the human mind. The mind, to the Romantics, was composed of many different faculties, chief among which were reason and imagination. The emotions were also an essential part of humanity. The aim of education was to develop and cultivate *all* these faculties in the individual. This could be done via the study of nature, mathematics, languages, history and literature. The centre of focus was, however, not the thing studied, but the student; not the object, but the subject.

The new Idea of a university was tied not only to psychology and aesthetics, but to political theories as well. Universities could bring about the education not only of individuals, but also of the entire human race. Fichte, Schelling, von Humboldt and Coleridge (among others) were all in agreement here. Universities could make society more moral, more cultured and (in Coleridge's eyes, at least) more Christian. None of these men envisaged mass university education. Instead, a core of cultured *Gelehrten*, or perhaps a godly clerisy, could be created to preserve civilization and combat social and moral ills.

The seed of this Idea was, in the cases of England and Germany, sown on two very different soils. Put more simply: England was a nation-state; Germany was not. England, particularly after the French revolution, felt very defensive about its national institutions, especially its Established Church and the two seminaries (Oxford and Cambridge) which produced clerics for that Church. Romantic thinkers varied in their assessment of the Tory politicians who governed England between 1798 and 1815, but, with notable exceptions, they came to support the Church and made no serious attempt to change the seminaries into secular institutions of higher learning.

If England felt defensive, Germany felt (for good reason) defeated. After Napoleon crushed the Prussian armies, German states attempted to fill the gaps left by political impotence with new adventures in the theory of the state and the Idea of a university. In the minds of German philosophers, the state gradually assumed a metaphysical importance which transcended the political realities of a weak, divided Germany. The state became 'world-historical', an embodiment of a great Spirit which governed human events. But how could such a state become real? How could a Germany which had known centuries of religious divisions and, now, conquest at the hand of an alien power be the source of such a state? To the Romantics, including Schiller, von Humboldt and others, the answer lay in *Bildung*, in the cultivation of beautiful souls through education. By discovering (and, in part, creating) their true selves, the young could become instruments of the World Spirit and builders of a great culture. This meant not merely a renewal of old universities (some of which were in French hands anyway), but the creation of new ones. These new universities would have an edge over those established in revolutionary France, for in them, young men would not learn to be better militarists or civil servants, but better thinkers and citizens. These universities, moreover, would create a new knowledge and would practise *Bildung durch Wissenschaft*, the cultivation of the young through the generation of new ideas. Both *Bildung* and *Wissenschaft* would serve the state; both would reveal the spirit behind the state as well.

To be sure, the English Romantics shared some notions with their German counterparts. To some extent they shared the desire to encourage self-development. More importantly, they also held the view that education must serve the state. But, as mentioned above, the English model was conservative; it was, moreover, explicitly religious in articulation. Oxford and Cambridge were seminaries, and this was fine indeed with Coleridge, Wordsworth and their followers. The German model, in contrast, was dynamic and metaphysical in articulation. Religion was certainly an underlying force, but it was schematized and purged of specifically Christian expression. Coleridge saw universities as places where young men learned to obey the Christian God and the God of Nature; the German reformers saw their institutions as places where a secularized World Spirit could grow into its own.

The Romantics – and their followers – have thus left a broad legacy for educational institutions throughout the western world. Where did it go? Fritz Ringer, in *The Decline of the German Mandarins*, argues convincingly that the original spirit of *Bildung durch Wissenschaft* became ossified and routinized by the rise of Teutonic scholarship as an instrument of German nationalism. The romantic

Idea of a university had a more conservative role in the reform of Oxford and Cambridge, for these universities did not change their direction until Parliament forced them to do so in the 1850s. Attempts were made before that date to reform these universities from within, and the products of these efforts, from tripos examinations to secret societies of learning, live on to this day. Perhaps the greatest impact Romanticism had in English universities was in preserving the colleges and the liberal arts curriculum from utilitarian assault.

But even if universities at the end of the nineteenth century were not what Romantics would have wanted, the romantic Idea of what they should have been remained. After all, an Idea calls people towards perfection, and perfection will ever elude academics as it does all mortals.

# 1

# The Confessional Idea of a University and its Fall, 1550–1750

> Once there were fine, resplendent times when Europe was a Christian land, when one Christendom occupied this humanly constituted continent. One great common interest united the remotest provinces of this broad spiritual realm. Without worldly possessions, one Head guided and unified the great political forces. A numerous guild, to which everyone had access, stood directly beneath him and carried out his behests and strove with zeal to confirm his beneficent power.[1]

So begins Novalis's mythic history of the western world, *Christendom or Europe*. This work presents the Middle Ages as the springtime of our civilization when Christ reigned through his holy minions and all was well with the world. Needless to say, Novalis makes no mention of the Albigensian Crusade, the Black Death, the Schism or other medieval unpleasantries; a romantic poet had no need for such mundane discomforts. But he does mention one thing which loosely corresponds with reality: the West knew one Church. This single Church controlled not only the guild of clerics, but also the guilds of teachers and scholars. From these guilds arose the university.

Universities, then, were confessional institutions, but since one religion dominated Western Europe, this confessionalism did not foster localism. Indeed, it encouraged just the opposite, for it enabled scholars to cross national boundaries with ease. William of Ockham, an Englishman, saw his ideas read on the continent. Thomas Aquinas, an Italian, taught at Paris. Scholars from Cambridge to Cracow spoke and read the *lingua franca*, Latin, and fiercely debated the same topics: whether the apostles had property; whether criminal clerics need be obeyed; whether universals exist; whether simple fornication was a sin. Students and scholars travelled frequently (often by foot), drank copiously and formed a truly international intellectual culture.

When the Reformation came in the sixteenth century, it brought in its wake a revision of the confessional Idea of a university. Europe was rent asunder, and the various confessions (Lutheran, Catholic, Calvinist, Anglican) struggled for survival and dominance. Universities became intellectual centres for this struggle. Their *raison d'être* was no longer to transmit a single Roman faith, but to propagate the state religion of a particular region. Whether Anglican, Lutheran, Calvinist or Roman Catholic, universities from 1550 until the eighteenth century were supposed to train clerics, combat the heresies of the other confessions and preserve the doctrines of whatever denomination they served. If *cuius regio* were indeed to have *eius religio*, if each region were to have its religion, then each domain would also have its universities.[2]

The Reformation, in fact, began in a university: Wittenberg. Luther did for the university what he did for church music – he retained many medieval forms, but employed them to promote the new evangelical faith. Latin remained the language of lectures. Theology was still the queen of sciences; logic remained scholastic and Aristotelian. But the supreme Head, the Pope, was replaced; from now on, the primary external influence on universities would be Germany's secular princes.

Among Lutheran universities, the greatest contributor to the curriculum was not Luther himself, but his friend, Melanchthon. One of Melanchthon's chief feats was maintaining a friendship with both Luther and Erasmus (which few others could). This willingness to accept humanism and attempt to marry it to the new faith revealed itself in his academic work. He served with distinction at Wittenberg for many years after Luther took it over, making it the academic centre of Protestant Germany. His system of organization and textbooks would dominate German universities for many decades to come.[3]

But politics as well as religion shaped the confessional Idea of a university. Universities produced the clerics needed to combat Romanism; they also gave each princeling the lawyers, doctors and civil servants needed in his state. Besides, a German ruler could find that his domain lay cheek by jowl with one ruled by a prince of another faith. One could hardly permit students in a Lutheran state to study under the Jesuits next door; by the same token, a Catholic prince had no desire to see his subjects educated by heretical Protestants. It only made sense to keep students from spending their gold abroad when they could just as well spend it at home.[4] The result was a spate of university foundations in sixteenth- and seventeenth-century Germany. Between 1527 and 1655, no fewer than nine new Protestant universities were founded in Germany, while over half a dozen Catholic ones came into existence during the same period.[5] But these numbers are a bit deceptive; as Paulsen notes, many of these institutions comprised only 10–12 professors, a few hundred students and a renovated convent.[6]

Given the increased tendency of students to stay in their own regions, the international aspect of study disappeared. Students no longer travelled as they once did. Indeed, by the end of the seventeenth century, more and more German princes forbad their subjects to study outside their realms. Instead of serving a universal Church, universities now existed to serve petty states and their particular confessions.

By the eighteenth century the two ancient universities of England were also clearly confessional in nature. Here, of course, there was only one sanctioned confession: the Church of England. Moreover, England's political unity prevented the multiplication of universities witnessed in Germany. Since there was only one state, there was no need for each region of the country to have a university.

If anything, though, universities in England had a stronger confessional identity than German ones. They were first and foremost seminaries for the Anglican Church. Few went there to study law or medicine; for such studies one went to the London Inns of Court or the Royal College of Surgeons (or went into a private apprenticeship). Non-Anglicans were *de facto* excluded from both universities. All matriculants at Oxford had to subscribe to the Thirty-nine Articles (the fundamental doctrinal statement of the Anglican faith) and all graduates from Cambridge had to do likewise. Between 1752 and 1765, moreover, 76 per cent of Cambridge graduates became clergymen.[7] Catholics and Protestant dissenters were not welcome, and all students were (in theory) in preparation for clerical careers.

As in Germany, this confessional Idea grew out of the Reformation. The statutes governing the universities were those imposed by Queen Elizabeth in an era when Popery seemed a real threat. And, as in Germany, a tie to the Church meant a tie to the state.

Cambridge graduates, for example, not only had to subscribe to the Thirty-nine Articles, but were also required to acknowledge the sovereign as Supreme Head of the Church.[8] In both Germany and England, then, universities were institutions expected to ally themselves with Church and State, to guard against the evils of heresy and to promote loyalty to the Crown. Their Idea, their purpose, was tied to the state confession.

The confessional Idea of a university grew out of an age of religious discord and functioned so long as ideological religious divisions were dominant. But what happened when the age of religious wars was past? Without religious conflict, what really was the purpose for universities? A look at the situation in the early to mid-eighteenth century may shed some light on these questions. We will begin with the situation in Germany.

Despite the Reformation, Protestant German universities held on to the structure bequeathed them by the Middle Ages. Most institutions retained four faculties: philosophy, law, medicine and theology. As in the past, the philosophy faculty (known in the Middle Ages as the *facultas artium*) was considered a lower faculty, while the other three were the upper ones. Only the upper faculties offered doctorates; Immanuel Kant, for example, never held this degree, but only a medieval-style licence to teach. By the eighteenth century it was not uncommon for students to rush through their courses in the philosophy faculty so they could quickly enter the professions. The bachelor's degree had fallen out of use and was generally not granted. Master's degrees were easy to get and meant little. Consequently, the only meaningful degree was the doctorate granted by the upper faculties.[9]

Of the upper faculties, the legal faculty was the strongest. The principalities of Germany needed civil servants. Young men seeking social and financial advancement could do no better than obtain training in the law. After all, what else could an ambitious man do than serve at court? He could, of course, go into the Church or medicine, but neither of these brought the social or financial rewards of the civil service. The medical faculties, though usually more active than those at Oxbridge, were in particularly low repute.[10]

No new confessional German universities were founded in the eighteenth century. The last confessional founding came late in the seventeenth century, at Halle. Even this school, as will be described in the next chapter, was different from its predecessors. The other schools continued, but intellectual life lost its edge. Gone were the days when universities were hotbeds of activity as in the age of Luther. Few students enrolled: between 1721 and 1730, the average enrolment at Jena was 1,446; in the decade following 1761 it fell to 703.[11] Even flagship institutions such as Halle and Göttingen had no more than 1,500 students at any given time.[12] Combined enrolments at all German universities averaged 8,000 to 9,000 between 1700 and 1755. Thereafter, they declined considerably until 1815.[13]

Those who came to the universities were notorious for their raucous behaviour. A new student could find his money taken away by fraternities who would then turn him over as a slave to an upperclassman.[14] Aristocratic students believed carrying a sword to be one of their privileges. Duelling continued, though after 1730, it was seldom fatal.[15] But the thing surest to drive students to riot was an increase in the price of beer. Pitched battles were not unknown between students and soldiers if the cost of this favourite German beverage increased.[16]

Rowdy students, though, were nothing new, nor would they go away after the eighteenth century passed. Even the young Friedrich Nietzsche bore a duelling scar on his face.[17] There was more amiss. The problem lay not just in declining enrolments or drunken students, but in the decline of the confessional Idea which justified the university's existence. No one illustrates this more clearly than Johann David Michaelis.

Michaelis (1717–91) was born and raised in the academic world. His father taught theology and oriental languages at Halle. Michaelis studied there, but came to the new University of Göttingen in 1745. In 1768, he published a lengthy, informative treatise entitled *Raissonement über die Protestantischen Universitäten in Deutschland* (Reasoning on the Protestant Universities in Germany). Perhaps even more than Michaelis realized, this book demonstrated why German universities were in trouble.

The treatise began by discussing why Germany had so many universities. The reason, Michaelis argued, was economic. Michaelis worked on a quasi-mercantilist economic principle, believing that states must endeavour to keep as much gold as possible within their borders. He estimated that a student without a scholarship spent about 300 thaler a year. If one kept 500 students at home (instead of letting them go abroad) the state would retain 150,000 thaler.[18] A university, then, could be a winning proposition for the small state, and Michaelis believed that was why so many states had opted for establishing one.

Michaelis also gave some advice on how to run a university. He advocated finding ways to please students with locally produced products. Local breweries, he argued, should brew the beer the students liked – that way, they would spend their money where they went to school, and not import foreign wines.[19] Besides stimulating the local beer industry, universities were great for the paper business. Most professors preferred to print locally. In the age of horsedrawn travel and unreliable posts, this made sense. Publishing a popular work could be quite lucrative; Halle, for example, earned a good deal from publishing a German translation of an English history text. But Michaelis regretted to inform his readers that the local prince could have managed things better, for he made the mistake of importing foreign paper, so halving his income from the deal.[20]

Michaelis, then, treated the university as a state business venture. His main concern was whether the university served the needs of the State. In taking this position, he practised *Kameralwissenschaft*, the science of running a court. He even went so far as to advocate closing down, for 'reasons of the State' (*Cameralgrudsätzen*), those universities that cost more than they drew in. 'He who wants to be a good housekeeper,' he argued, 'will be he who counts.'[21] But the counting must be done by the prince's own officials and not by the professors: the professors would inflate their accounts since they had an interest in keeping the school open.[22] Indeed, sometimes a Latin school made more sense than a university, for younger students would not send their money abroad to purchase foreign luxuries.[23] Michaelis's rule was always the same: he who kept the most gold within his borders won.

Michaelis then went to a question openly debated in eighteenth-century Germany: why not close *all* universities? After all, Athens had no need of them,[24] and some argued that young men should study on their own under good supervision rather than trouble with the antiquated formality of universities.[25] But Michaelis rejected these claims, asserting instead that universities brought great things to the states that nurtured them. He said that there was more to running a university than if it were merely 'a factory, or a glassworks'.[26] 'A well-run university,' he went on, 'primarily brings with it the great good, that sciences and arts bloom in the land.'[27] This blooming was, in turn, good for the political strength of the State. Even the teaching of theology served the State by combating religious discord.[28] And even though numerous universities existed in Germany, states should consider supporting their own since they might have peculiar educational needs. Coastal states might, for example, needed to train students in navigation, while inland states did not. Michaelis called the failure of Oxbridge to teach navigation 'an unforgivable sin of the universities against the state'.[29]

Universities, then, should exist, but only to serve the State's needs. Note the emphasis on the needs of the *State*, not the *Church*. The universities were, as Michaelis's title suggests, Protestant universities, but they were really the universities of Protestant princes. They were not there to evangelize or eradicate the scourge of Romanism. Nor were they there to promote new learning:

> The betterment of sciences, and the making of new discoveries, is not really the duty of a school, whether they be lower or higher. It is instead the affair of gifted individuals, or . . . of scientific societies.[30]

The confessional Idea of Melanchthon and Luther was gone; in its place was not an educational Idea, nor a broad-based justification for the university's existence, but an admonition to watch the balance sheet. Michaelis presented a narrow, *Kleinstaat*-centred theory of why universities existed. But he believed that Germany needed universities anyway, because nothing else could take their place. He observed that 'we have no London, no Paris' and consequently no place for the learned or literary to gather together.[31]

Such, of course, was not the case in England. By the mid-eighteenth century, London boasted a fine literary culture with the likes of James Boswell, Dr Johnson and Oliver Goldsmith enjoying one another's company in coffee houses and pubs. Fleet Street produced books of varying quality on a myriad of topics. Whatever one wanted, one could find somewhere in England's capital – anything from cheap pornography to Pope, Dryden or Fielding.

But what of England's universities? They played a different role from their German counterparts. First of all, England's political unity prevented the multiplication of universities witnessed in Germany. Instead of each tiny region having a university of its own, England had only two. These institutions, moreover, were purely seminaries and aristocratic finishing schools and did not generate doctors or lawyers as Jena or Halle did. Hardly anyone studied law or medicine at Oxbridge; these faculties existed only as shadows of the medieval past. Almost all students took degrees in the arts faculty.

In 1800, Cambridge granted nine degrees in law, 19 in theology, four in medicine, and 161 (81 A.M., 80 B.A.) in arts.[32] Even though all graduates were supposed to enter orders, few seriously studied theology.

Politics played a key role in eighteenth-century Oxbridge. The Anglican Church was, after all, a State Church in need of defence against the State's political enemies. Indeed, W. R. Ward gives the impression that politics far outweighed education. Ward's opinion may be due to his own predilection for political history, but one statement of his merits repeating:

> No serious study of the reasons for the academic decline of Oxford in the middle of the eighteenth century has ever been attempted, but among them must be reckoned the sacrifice made to politics in these years, sacrifices which the university as a school of the Church in a time when political and ecclesiastical disputes were not readily distinguished, could hardly avoid making.[33]

Oxford suffered particularly due to the government's long-standing suspicion that it was a Jacobite stronghold. Oxford was undeniably a Tory bastion, and the Whigs feared it so much that troops were quartered there during the 1715 Jacobite uprising.[34] But were political squabbles with the government the only problem? Probably not: Cambridge was loyally Whig, but, judging from D. A. Winstanley's account in *Unreformed Cambridge* (an account largely supported by the new history of Cambridge), it was hardly a better place to study than Oxford. There was more than political wrangling behind the decline of the university – there was a decline of enrolment, curricula, professors and colleges. What lay behind this decline was the gradual loss of the confessional Idea of a university and the failure of a new one to replace it.

Judging from matriculation records, enrolments declined considerably at Oxford in the eighteenth century. Between 1660 and 1700, matriculations there averaged 435 a year. The decline in the eighteenth century was noticeable: from 1701 to 1750 matriculations averaged 265; from 1751 to 1800 they dropped to 233.[35] Cambridge enrolment figures were similarly grim; indeed, as late as 1755, Cambridge could claim only 736 undergraduates on record.[36] Contemporary accounts indicate that many who came did not graduate. Some, such as Dr. Johnson, left Oxford due to poverty. Charles

Fox, on the other hand, left to go on the Grand Tour. Others went down without taking a degree because they did not wish to enter into holy orders. Unlike in the present age, England in the eighteenth century did not expect a successful young man to have a degree. He did not need to go to university at all; and if he did, he did not need to graduate.

For those matriculants who chose to take a B.A. the demands of Oxbridge were not rigorous. Once, in 1784, a French student visiting Cambridge inquired from the Regius Professor of Modern History about Cambridge's course of study. The professor answered with complete sincerity that he knew nothing about it.[37] The professor cannot be faulted on this score. The statutory requirements for graduation had remained unchanged from the days of Elizabeth, and were, in fact, medieval in origin. To become a bachelor of arts, the University of Cambridge required that a student (1) complete twelve terms of residency; (2) pass some *viva voce* exercises called 'Acts and Opponencies'; (3) be admitted in the twelfth term 'ad respondendum quaestioni' (responding to questions, in this case, questions from Aristotle); and (4) go through a period of exercises called 'standing in quadragesima'.[38]

So read the statutes. In reality, many of these requirements had fallen into disuse at Cambridge. The requirements of twelve terms' residency, for example, became *de facto* one of ten terms. Often students could be credited for a term of residence even if they spent whole weeks of the term in London frequenting taverns and coffee houses. Of the exercises and examinations listed above, only the 'Acts and Opponencies' were performed with any regularity. These were a throwback to the medieval disputation. A student would be challenged to debate a proposition, and the debate would be judged by a fellow acting as moderator. The disputants employed Aristotelian, syllogistic logic and argued strictly in Latin. A century later, William Whewell observed that in these student debates, 'the syllogisms were such as would make Aristotle stare, and the Latin would make every classical hair on your head stand on end...'[39] So an undergraduate could achieve a degree by spending five to seven weeks a term at Cambridge for ten terms, learning some basic Aristotelian logic and mastering Latin. Since most would have learned Latin before coming to university, Cambridge made very modest demands of them indeed.

There were none the less additional rewards for the industrious at eighteenth-century Oxbridge. At Cambridge, the honours tripos in mathematics was quite competitive and an honours degree could open the doors to the best clerical preferments. While Cambridge as yet had no tripos in classics (and would not until 1822), some scholars genuinely coveted the medal given each year to the finest classicist. Not all students at Oxbridge were slothful; some used the flexible curriculum to their advantage and learned modern languages, Hebrew, Arabic and the natural sciences. Charles Darwin and William Wordsworth were both outstanding examples of such self-motivated students.[40] But such scholars obtained a good education in spite of the system, not because of it.

One of the abler students of Oxford was Jeremy Bentham. Born in 1748 into a Jacobite family, Bentham began to study Latin at five years of age. He attended Westminster and went up to Queen's College, Oxford, when he was only twelve. He took 60 books with him, of which only twelve were in English. Bentham immediately encountered two common bugbears when he entered Oxford: the Thirty-nine Articles and a tutor.

Like all Oxford matriculants, Bentham had to subscribe to the Thirty-nine Articles of the Church of England. But he was unable (in contrast to many of his contemporaries) simply to sign them and forget about it. 'In some of them,' he related later, 'no meaning at all could I find; in others no meaning but one which, in my eyes, was but plainly irreconcilable either to reason or to scripture.'[41] Queen's College had a fellow who specialized in soothing tender consciences on these matters; by and by, this fellow had his way and Bentham signed. Being a scrupulous person, Bentham regretted his subscription to the Articles for the rest of his life and considered it an act of hypocrisy. He later wrote a treatise about how such false swearing ruined the moral integrity of the universities.

Bentham saw his tutor, a Mr. Jefferson, as an intrusive meddler in his education. According to Bentham, the only reason his father hired Jefferson was that he charged only six guineas a year while his rival charged eight. Bentham described Jefferson as 'sour and repulsive – a sort of Protestant monk'.[42] The tutor offered little new to the precocious youth. Jefferson assigned Cicero's orations, the Greek Testament (which Bentham already knew) and a smattering of textbook philosophy and logic. He did not help Bentham at all with mathematics; his studies in this field were all self-directed. Bentham none the less did stay long enough to take a degree in 1763 at the age of 16.

Another famous young Oxford matriculant of this era was Edward

Gibbon. He came up to Magdalen College in 1752 when he was only 14. Like Bentham, he had already done a good deal of studying, especially in history. He later noted:

> I arrived at Oxford with a stack of erudition that might have puzzled a Doctor and a degree of ignorance of which a school boy would have been ashamed.[43]

Gibbon also shared Bentham's bad experience with the tutorial system. He claimed that his first tutor presented no plan of study except for the reading of Terence's comedies. Gibbon's second tutor did even less, and Gibbon blamed the indifference of this tutor for his brief lapse into Roman Catholicism. This falling away from the Church of England brought Gibbon's university career to an abrupt end.[44] 'I spent fourteen months at Magdalen College,' he wrote, 'they proved the fourteen months the most idle and unprofitable of my life.'[45] Gibbon's cynicism about Oxford remains infamous and is best summed up when he declared:

> To the university of Oxford I acknowledge no obligation; and she will as cheerfully renounce me as a son as I am willing to disclaim her for a mother.[46]

While pursuing his personalized attack on Oxford, Gibbon tried to offer an explanation for the university's weakness. Some of his complaints sound familiar: professors did not teach; fellows and students were idle drunkards. But a few stand out as more important; namely, that the English universities were trapped in the medieval past, and that their financial policies did not encourage teaching.

Much of Gibbon's assault on the medieval aspects of the universities probably stems from his well-known antipathy to religion. But there was more to it than that: his attack also demonstrated how the Enlightenment had passed English universities by. 'The Arts,' according to Gibbon,

> are supposed to include the liberal knowledge of Philosophy and literature; but I am informed that some tattered shreds of the old Logic and Metaphysics compose the exercises for a Batchelor [*sic*] and Master's degree . . .[47]

As indicated by the above discussion about Cambridge, Gibbon's statement would appear to have been applicable to both universities. The knowledge which he considered important, especially the new philosophy of Locke and Hume or the wisdom of Goldsmith or Fielding, was altogether absent from the Oxbridge curriculum. The British Enlightenment came from Edinburgh and London, not Oxford and Cambridge. The Enlightenment had not given the English universities a new sense of purpose, so the universities relied on one from their religious past.

The situation was very different north of the Cheviots, especially in Edinburgh. While the University of Edinburgh had been established by the city as a confessional institution in 1582, it had become something very different by the mid-eighteenth century. While it remained loyal to the Kirk of Scotland, it had become a world-class institution and a centre for the Enlightenment. Using the Dutch universities as its model, it abandoned the tutorial system early in the century and embraced the continental habit of professorial teaching, supported in this instance largely by lecture fees collected directly from students. In the arts faculty, chairs were established in Greek, several branches of philosophy, history, rhetoric and belles-lettres. The medical faculty was second to none, and had the first chair of anatomy (established in 1705) anywhere in the British Isles.[48] By the late eighteenth century, Edinburgh had granted over 100 medical doctorates and drew medical students from England and even the fledgling United States. Many of Edinburgh's products became the makers of the Scottish Enlightenment, including David Hume, Oliver Goldsmith, the founders of the *Edinburgh Review* and James Mill.[49]

Another famed member of the Scottish Enlightenment, Adam Smith, offered a critique of Oxbridge based in part from his knowledge of Scottish universities. Smith presents the rare case of a Scotsman with an English education. Most Scots seeking higher education preferred to go to a Scottish university. However, there were a few who went to Oxbridge, especially from Episcopal families. Such was the case with Smith, who won an exhibition to Balliol College, Oxford, in 1740. All who won this exhibition were required by statute to take orders in the Scottish Episcopal Church – a requirement that was poorly enforced after the Act of Union and that Smith evaded even though he took a degree. Smith spent six years at Oxford (1740–46); later, he accepted the chair of moral philosophy at Glasgow and lectured on ethics, rhetoric and belles-lettres.

As one might expect, Smith examined universities from an economic point of view. In *The Wealth of Nations* he observed that universities relied on two sources of income: fees charged to students and endowments. Smith contended that endowments, instead of promoting good education, had ruined pedagogy in the English universities. Competition, he contended, brought out the best in teachers as it did in businessmen. It would guarantee that good courses would be offered and taught in an effective way. 'Rivalship and emulation render excellency', and such 'excellency' would lead to education in subjects which students needed for their own self interest.[50]

But such competition did not exist at Oxbridge. Instead of having to compete for students, Oxbridge professors received a fixed salary funded by an endowment. The result was that 'in the university of Oxford, the greater part of the public professors have, for these many years, given up altogether even the pretence of teaching.'[51] Professors, moreover, could not be forced to teach by the university authorities. University statutes could (and, in fact, did) demand that professors give lectures, but no law or statute could force a professor to lecture well.[52] As mentioned above, such statutes were routinely ignored anyway. Endowments thus functioned like the monopolies of the mercantile system. They artificially protected professors from the laws of supply and demand and allowed academic failures to survive without rewarding the worthy.

Why, then, did the young bother to go to university? As the statistics cited above suggest, many indeed did not. But the universities were still a means to clerical and social preferment, and a degree could lead to a comfortable life as a fellow or vicar. And here, argued Smith, lay another reason why the universities were so weak. Professors lived on fixed salaries from endowments and taught (or were supposed to teach) students who came not to get an education but to get on in the world. The English universities had a captive audience so that the institutions themselves, like the instructors in them, were artificially sheltered from the intellectual market place.

Smith sharply contrasted this situation with that of higher education in antiquity. The sophists of old relied entirely on payments from students for their survival. They had no authority over students, no protection from unemployment, no captive audience. In such circumstances, they had to teach useful things and teach them well. If modern professors were likewise thrust into an open, competitive market, they, too, would teach what students needed to know.[53]

Smith thus offered an Idea for the university based on utility. Instead of remaining aloof from changes in society, universities should become an integral part of the world around them. It was the growing sense that Oxford and Cambridge were not useful – that they were centres of antiquated learning and sloth – which would, in the next century, be a force behind the move to take them away from the Church of England and put them into secular hands. The utilitarian Idea of a university, here presaged by Smith, would eventually be the main opponent in England to the romantic Idea of a university.

But much as Gibbon and Smith foreshadowed the utilitarian Idea of a university, so did John Wesley the Romantic. In Wesley, one finds the same appeal to religion and to institutional conservatism which later became apparent in the likes of Coleridge and Whewell.

Unlike Gibbon and Smith, Wesley had a deep-seated affection for the ancient English universities. He confessed to having 'a prejudice in favour of our universities, that of Oxford in particular' and said:

> I love the very sight of Oxford; I love the manner of life; I love and esteem many of its institutions.[54]

Oxford retained a special place in his heart. This grew out of the special religious experiences which he had there, experiences which set Wesley on his way as the founder of the most remarkable British religious movement of the century.

Wesley came up to Christ's Church, Oxford, in 1720. At 17, he was older than Bentham and Gibbon, but, like them, he had already gained considerable knowledge, especially in languages. He had some misgivings about the Calvinist, predestinarian aspects of the Thirty-nine Articles but subscribed to them anyway. Unlike any of the other English figures examined so far, Wesley took orders after he graduated and did so willingly. He was elected a fellow at Lincoln College and was eventually made Greek lecturer and moderator there.

As a fellow, Wesley took his academic responsibilities seriously. He moderated disputations often and kept himself on a regular schedule of study. He devoted Mondays and Tuesdays to classics, Wednesdays to logic and ethics, Thursdays to Hebrew and Arabic, Fridays to metaphysics, Saturdays to orations and poetry, and Sundays to divinity. As time went on, though, his studies became less broad. His growing dedication to the Bible crowded out other things. One companion warned him that 'the Bible knows nothing of solitary religion', and Wesley took the words to heart.[55] He sought out and found a few others, mostly undergraduates, who would join him in Bible study and prayers. Here, even before his famous meeting with the Moravians, began Wesley's career as an evangelical.

Given the atmosphere of religious cynicism and hypocrisy then prevalent at Oxford, Wesley quickly found himself a *vox clamantis in deserto*. His band of fifteen or so fasted and studied divinity. They set up a scheme of self-examination for their souls. Some ridiculed them and called them 'Bible bigots' and 'the Holy', yet the name which stuck was 'Methodist'.[56] Wesley had done what the Cambridge Apostles and the Oxford Tractarians would do in the nineteenth century. Since the existing curriculum did not offer enough in divinity, they set out to study it on their own and established a separate society within the university to do so. Like these later groups, the Oxford Methodists were not trying to reform the entire university; instead, they sought to educate each other.

Georgian Oxford was simply not ready for such a club. If they had merely gone drinking and hunting, allowances could have been made for them. But the Methodists were guilty of far greater crimes: they were devout and, worst of all, anti-social. Wesley and his followers fell out of favour with the university authorities. The Seniors of Christ's Church held a meeting to discuss the 'enthusiasm' of Wesley and his followers.[57] Rumours spread that the university would step in to break up the club, and that one of its members had fasted to death with Wesley's encouragement. All of this innuendo reduced membership in the club until, by 1734, only five or so remained in it.

Wesley knew it was time to leave Oxford. He wrote to his father that 'God made us for a social life, and to this academical studies are only preparatory'.[58] His family wanted him to use the means of escape customary for an Oxford fellow: take up a clerical living. His father had not long to live and could arrange for Wesley to take over his position at Epworth. But Wesley chose his own path and opted to do missionary work in the colonies. Here, of course, he had his famous meeting with the German Moravians. But as is evidenced by his Oxford experiences, his leaning towards evangelical enthusiasm appeared long before his heart was 'strangely warmed' in 1738.

Years later Wesley established a school of his own; in the process of doing so, he made several illuminating observations about English universities. His Kingswood school, located a few miles outside Bristol, began operations in 1748. It was designed primarily to offer a godly and disciplined education to the children of the area's colliers. Some of its students went on to Oxford with Wesley's encouragement, but they encountered resistance from the university community. An anti-Methodist mood still prevailed, and six of the Kingswood graduates were expelled.

Wesley then suggested that the Methodists follow in the footsteps of the older dissenting sects and establish an academy of their own. His proposal was to offer a four-year term in higher study. Kingswood, he argued, could do a better job of teaching than Oxford. Despite his above-cited affection for Oxford, Wesley observed that the university's tutors were 'utterly unqualified for the work . . . being far from masters even of Latin and Greek, and ignorant of the very elements of the sciences.'[59] Due to numerous administrative problems at Kingswood this upper course was never offered. After all, Wesley himself never broke entirely from the Church of England. He only departed from its structure when he felt it necessary to serve his goals (such as when he preached out of doors or consecrated his own bishops). He saw Oxbridge's limitations, but baulked at breaking entirely from these special institutions of the Established Church.

Wesley's acceptance of the religious role of the universities is what sets him apart from Bentham, Gibbon and Smith. His religious beliefs encouraged him to see the spiritual, as opposed to the utilitarian, value of these institutions. Even if their teachers were not of the highest calibre, they at least gave a young man time to study ancient languages and the word of God. But Wesley, like Smith and the others, did not offer a close critical examination of the Oxbridge curriculum. Such an examination came from a now-forgotten figure named Vicesimus Knox.

Knox's life revolved around education. Born in Middlesex in 1752, his father served as a Master of Tunbridge School. Knox went up to Oxford in 1771, took a B.A. in 1775, and served as a fellow there for four years. He then succeeded his father as master of Tunbridge and died in 1821. A prolific and popular writer, he published (among other things) *Liberal Education: or, a Practical Treatise on the Methods of Acquiring Useful and Polite Learning* (1781). This work was an enormous success and rapidly went through ten editions.

*Liberal Education* dealt with just that: what a liberal education was to a Georgian. Knox spent much of the first volume discussing the general aspects of liberal education and devoted most of the second to the universities. Of these institutions, Knox stated in his preface:

> I chiefly, though not entirely, allude to that of Oxford, of which I am an useless member . . . As this part of my work cannot fail of giving offence to some, I hope I may be permitted to declare, that my animadversions on the universities arise from pure motives.[60]

Knox clearly had an image in mind of what a liberal education entailed. Note that his work was a 'practical guide' to getting 'useful and polite' learning. He eschewed the work of Locke, Milton and (particularly) Rousseau as 'impractical', arguing that 'when they have written on education, they have fallen into the common error of those who attend to speculation more than to practice.'[61] Unlike any of these men (or, for that matter, Gibbon) Knox spent his entire life as a professional educator and this showed in his book.

Knox did not advocate a radical revision of the curriculum, but merely wanted the curriculum purified of superficialities and false-hoods. 'I mean, then,' he wrote, 'to speak in favour of that ancient system of education, which consists in a classical discipline, and which has produced in our nation many ornaments of human nature.'[62] Reading Greek and Roman writers would build the morals of students, producing 'sentiments and notions no less liberal and enlarged than elegant and ingenious'.[63] He noted that some considered such an education useless, but dismissed such sceptics as men who failed ever to obtain an education themselves.

Knox valued knowledge for its own sake and for the beneficial effects it would have on the mind. He contrasted narrow, professionally-oriented education (which, he implied, was the growing norm of his day) with what he considered true liberal learning:

> There are, I think, two kinds of education; one of them confined, the other enlarged; one, which only tends to qualify for a particular sphere of action, for a profession, or an official employment; the other, which endeavours to improve the powers of understanding for their own sake; for the sake of exalting the endowments of human nature, and rendering it capable of sublime and refined contemplation.[64]

Coleridge or Fichte would have firmly agreed with this statement, and may even have worded their opinions similarly. This emphasis on 'exalting' the mind to 'sublime' contemplation fitted well with some aspects of romantic thought. Knox was no Romantic, but the criteria he used for judging universities contain some aspects of the romantic Idea of a university.

Knox found the English universities of his day sorely wanting. He noted that many wealthy families no longer bothered with them, resorting instead to private tutelage and the Grand Tour to educate their sons.[65] Knox was so disillusioned with Oxbridge that he did not think this was necessarily a bad idea. Since the universities were 'favourable to the diffusion of ignorance, idleness, vice, and infidelity' instead of knowledge and good morals, perhaps it was better to send the young to a good quiet town with books and tutor.[66] Knox also entertained the notion of breaking up the universities and dispersing the various colleges throughout the kingdom.[67] He insisted that if anyone went to university in England despite his warnings, he must secure a private tutor. Only in this way could he be guaranteed an adequate education. The universities themselves could offer opulent buildings and good libraries, but little else. To the average mind they could be mere sinkholes of temptation; to the superior intellect, they became prisons:

> Some very eminent POETS have not, however, been very fond of the universities. Witness Milton and Grey, cum multis aliis. The fettering of such men with statutes, disputations, etc. was like confining an eagle in a cage.[68]

Yet Knox swore that he did not wish to see universities abolished – only reformed. He continually attacked those who wished to abolish universities and defended their existence. But this defence lacked real enthusiasm, and Knox was much more critical of English universities than Michaelis was of German ones.

Knox joined in the chorus of those who criticized English professors. He quoted one Dr. Newton, Principal of Hartford College, who wrote of professors in the Georgian age:

> I have known a profligate debauchee chosen professor of moral philosophy; and a fellow who never looked upon the stars soberly in his life, professor of astronomy.[69]

Ward reports on a Regius professor of medicine, Dr. Hoy, who did absolutely nothing. Instead, he left the work to a deputy, who, in turn, left it to yet another deputy. The situation became untenable when Dr. Hoy's deputy died while Dr. Hoy was in Jamaica. No one could be appointed to the position because it was not officially vacant, so the professorship remained in limbo for six years until Dr. Hoy finally resigned. In the interim, no teaching of any kind came out of the professorship.[70]

Things were little better at Cambridge. The Knightbridge professor of moral theology was bound by statute to lecture five times a term in Latin. But in fact no one lectured at all, until well into the nineteenth century. In 1850 William Whewell testified that no holder of this professorship before himself ever lectured.[71]

Knox, moreover, agreed that the colleges failed to fill the pedagogical gap left by lazy professors. Colleges failed in their duty to supply students with a morally sound environment. Here, of course, English universities took on a responsibility which German ones did not event pretend to accept. Germany students lived (and still live) largely on their own, scattered throughout a university town. German universities left them to their own devices when it came to housing and the regulation of their lives. But English universities did not, for they insisted on housing students together in colleges with fellows and tutors.

In the eighteenth century, these fellows contributed little to the welfare of students. Knox said that colleges were given to 'vulgar enjoyments', and that the lectures of tutors were 'short, perfunctory, and of little use to real students'.[72] Gibbon fully agreed with this assessment; as a gentleman-commoner he was permitted to spend some time with fellows, but found them 'stagnated in a round of college business, Tory politics, personal stories, and private scandal'.[73]

The result of this neglect, claimed Knox, was the failure of colleges not only to educate young men, but to oversee their moral welfare. Knox reminded the reader that these universities were seminaries, but noted that

> in no place of education are young men more extravagant; in none do they catch the contagion of admiring hounds and horses to so violent a degree. . . . in none can they be less soberly brought up to the sacred function or to any other useful or honourable employment.[74]

Knox even went so far as to blame the prevailing moral laxness of his age on the universities. 'I verily believe,' he continued,

> that much of the corruption of morals, and unbelief of religion, which is now visible throughout the nation, is derived from the ignorance, carelessness, and vice of clergyman trained in the universities of England. The foul fountain has poured its polluted stream over the country; the people have tasted and have been poisoned with the draught.[75]

Here Knox was ascribing to the universities a task which, several generations later, Coleridge would demand of them: that they be the guardians of the nation's morals. But Knox found them sorely wanting in their fulfilment of this duty. He also argued that they failed to teach young men to be gentlemen, and even admitted that the best means of becoming a gentleman might have been outside the university. Herein might be a clue to the cause of the decline of universities in the eighteenth century.

What was wrong was that the old, confessional Idea of a university had ceased to function, but a new Idea had yet to replace it. In his fine work *Tradition and Change in English Liberal Education*, Sheldon Rothblatt examines what the term 'liberal education' meant in the Georgian age. He notes that

> The history of a liberal education in Georgian England is truly a history of the science of right living. It is the history of socio-moral conduct.[76]

It is the story, says Rothblatt, of acquiring the ability to lead a polite, civilized life in the world at large; in short, how to be a gentleman. Even Knox would concur in part with Rothblatt's assessment, for while Knox advocated learning for its own sake (and thus argued for a heavy emphasis on classics in the curriculum), he none the less believed that

> Every scholar ought to be a gentleman; and indeed I can hardly conceive a true gentleman . . . who is not in some degree, a polite scholar.[77]

But where in the Augustan age would one go to become a gentleman? To London, of course. London became more conscious of its role as a cultural, urban centre.[78] It was here that gentleman were fashioned. Given the peculiar requirements for residency at Oxford and Cambridge (students were required to be in residence only a few weeks each term), even university students spent much of their time and money in London. And many young would-be gentlemen never bothered to go to university at all, for as Rothblatt observes:

> In the eighteenth century a liberal education did not assume and certainly did not require residence at a university.[79]

In England, liberal education of this sort took place in London's inns, coffeehouses and theatres. It could be obtained through a dissenting academy, through reading classical authors on one's own or through conversation in the great *salons* on the continent. Due to the lack of any real urban centres in Germany, universities there faced the need to offer this type of education, but their declining enrolments and the open discussion of closing them down indicates that they were not effective in doing so.

This age demanded the education of the Enlightenment, one in which good breeding counted for everything. The university, still tied to a vestigial confessional Idea, had little to offer this generation. Michaelis complained that Tübingen 'had too much left over from the cloister', while an English don opined that Oxford and Cambridge 'have been too much permitted to creep on in the same lazy channel which was marked out for them in the days of Gothic ignorance'.[80] Gibbon repeatedly decried the ties of English universities to the medieval Church, with the retention of celibacy for fellows and Aristotelian logic in the disputation. With the supposed progress of civilization out of confessionalism and into the age of secularist Enlightenment, the old confessional *raison d'être* of universities had ceased to function. 'Nothing is wanting,' said one Cambridge fellow, 'but a power to give their waters new directions, in order to fertilize every quarter of useful knowledge.'[81]

But from where would this push come? Rothblatt argues that not one, but several competing theories of education would arise at the end of the eighteenth century.[82] One would be the utilitarian ethos arising from industrialism; but another would grow from Romanticism, the self-conscious reaction against the Enlightenment and the eighteenth century.

# 2
# The Genesis of the Romantic Idea of a University in Germany

As we saw in chapter 1, universities in England and Germany experienced considerable difficulty in the late eighteenth century. This chapter deals with the complex array of ideas present in German academic circles at the end of the eighteenth century, and pays particular attention to how three strains came together at Jena in the 1790s to give rise to the romantic Idea of a university. These strains were the renewal of interest in philology and classical studies at Halle and Göttingen, the idealist philosophy of Immanuel Kant and the neo-humanist ethos of Goethe and the court at Weimar.

Throughout the period under discussion, reform of German universities came not only by reforming existing institutions, but also by setting up new ones. Two such new establishments came at Halle (established in 1694) and Göttingen (established in 1737). In many ways, Halle offered little that was new. It aimed at creating the pool of *Beamter* (civil servants) which the courts of Germany needed for tax collection, running the law courts and maintaining the Lutheran Church. The upper faculties (law, theology and medicine) lent their aid to this cause, while the lower arts faculty served mainly as a preparation for professional studies. Students matriculated immediately into one of the upper faculties, and often gave short shrift to their studies in the arts and sciences.[1] One must remember that not only lawyers but also doctors and (in Protestant areas) ministers were all servants of the myriad petty despots of the empire. And Halle was just the school for them: career-oriented, with a special emphasis on the *Kameralwissenschaften*, the practical sciences of running a court.[2]

Perhaps the one person of note from Halle was Christian Wolff, whose writings dominated German academe after 1750 much as

Paley's ideas were to dominate Cambridge half a century later. Wolff was first and foremost a man of the Enlightenment. After studying at Leipzig, he won his chair at Halle thanks largely to a good word from Leibniz.[3] While there, he lectured in mathematics and philosophy. He was perhaps best known for his metaphysics, which confidently presented proofs of the existence of God which Kant would later dismiss. Wolff accepted previous ontological proofs for God's existence. He placed an even greater emphasis on cosmological proofs, arguing that the world required a sufficient reason to exist, and that this reason was the divine will.[4] These arguments would make him famous – and get him fired. The theology faculty at Halle, dominated by Lutherans of a Pietist bent, frowned on speculations about God, believing that God could be known only by faith. Due in large part to their protests, Wolff was dismissed in 1739. He was a martyr for the Enlightenment, and one of Frederick the Great's first acts of state was to return this oppressed friend of reason to his chair, where Wolff remained with growing fame and influence until his death in 1754.

Wolff contributed to reform of German universities in several ways. First, his reinstatement and subsequent appointment as dean of German philosophy demonstrated the desire of the Enlightenment to give German universities a more secular character. Wolff, moreover, symbolized the growing hopes for *Lehrfreiheit* (freedom of teaching), particularly since he taught in the lower, philosophical faculty.[5] But despite his clash with officialdom, he demonstrated no great interest in changing the way in which German universities were run, or limiting the power of German princes over them.[6]

More basic changes in the Idea of a university came about after the founding of the University of Göttingen in 1737. Its creators envisaged another training ground for civil servants, but things did not go as planned. Two distinguished professors in the lower faculty helped turn Göttingen away from the usual track of career preparation, and towards something resembling a modern German university. One, J. M. Gesner, made study of classical languages and literature a central part of his curriculum, aiming to train the intellectual and moral qualities of his students.[7] His successor, C. G. Heyne, was one of the first instructors to use the seminar system in place of the medieval disputation. Heyne's seminar in philology achieved considerable fame, and contributed to the close, *wissenschaftlich* (broadly, 'scientific') study of classical and oriental texts which continued in Germany into the nineteenth century.

Heyne's efforts contributed to the new sense of how German academics felt universities should be run. For one thing, the concept of knowledge as an end in itself, and the goal of cultivating young minds, began to eclipse the previous emphasis on training for a profession. The focus of attention for reformers went from the higher faculties to the lower one, from medicine, law and theology to literature, philology and philosophy. Moreover, it was in the lower faculty that the ideal of academic freedom could develop. But the cause of the lower faculty – and with it, of the triumph of a new type of philosophy – would be taken up at the end of the eighteenth century in the Prussian University of Königsberg by its resident sage, Immanuel Kant.

When Kant arrived in 1740, the University of Königsberg did not stand out from its counterparts in other German dominions. As the son of a local saddle-maker, Kant probably could not have afforded to go to another university; moreover, Prussia, like other German states, had laws restricting study elsewhere. Like most other German institutions of its day, Königsberg stressed teaching far above research and aimed primarily at getting students into their chosen professions.[8] One should bear in mind that the lower faculty taught not only philosophy, but other arts and sciences as well; at Königsberg, the lower faculty had eight regular chairs, and one extraordinary professor each in Hebrew, mathematics, Greek, logic and metaphysics, practical philosophy (that is, ethics), oratory and history, natural science and poetics.[9] Moreover, professors sometimes taught several subjects; Kant's favourite instructor, Martin Knutzen, taught his charge not only Wolffian metaphysics, but also mathematics and Newtonian physics.[10] Kant himself later taught geography as well as philosophy.

Until he won international renown as a scholar, Kant's life at Königsberg was one of poverty and obscurity. He served for a time as a private tutor to a wealthy family, a position offering little more status than did domestic service. Other famous academics of the eighteenth century, including J. G. Fichte and Adam Smith, likewise found that reduced circumstances forced them into such work, which many of them hated. In 1755, Kant returned to the university as a *Privatdozent*, and remained there for the rest of his life. He stayed a mere *Dozent* for fifteen years, and was twice denied a professorship until he won a chair in logic and metaphysics in 1770. From that point his fame grew; by the time his *Critique of Pure Reason* appeared in 1781, he was by far the most renowned professor at Königsberg. The universities of Halle, Jena and Erlangen all tried to woo him away from his home town, and Kant's fame put the University of Königsberg firmly on the academic map of Germany.

While he was a vital, creative new force in philosophy, there is little indication that Kant was adventurous in the lecture hall. He did not use the seminar format then being developed at Göttingen, but taught in the traditional style of lectures and disputations. Moreover he used the same textbooks – those required by the Prussian bureau of education – throughout his long career.[11] In his lectures, however, he was not slavish to the texts; notwithstanding the opacity of most of his extant prose, he had a reputation as a witty and informative lecturer.

Kant was, above all else, a conscious participant in the Enlightenment. This applied as much to his writings on education as anything else. None the less his thoughts about higher education and the university contributed to the rise of the romantic Idea of the university at Jena. In educational theory, as in other areas of inquiry, Paulsen's assessment of Kant makes sense:

> If we wish to describe Kant's position in a single formula we may say that he is at once the finisher and conqueror of the Illumination.[12]

Kant brought into his discussion of higher education the rationalistic approach typical of the Enlightenment. He also helped contribute to the growth of the role of the professor and the lower faculty which continued at Jena and Berlin.

At the bottom of it all lay Kant's intense belief in the need to subordinate everything to reason. To Kant, philosophy was 'the science of the relation of all cognition to the essential aims of reason'.[13] Kant's most famous works, including the *Critique of Pure Reason* and his *Prolegomena to Any Future Metaphysics*, sought to reduce all philosophy, and particularly metaphysics and ethics, to a science; or rather, to lay the foundations for continued *wissenschaftlich*, or 'scientific', inquiry into philosophical questions. This position gave Kant a sense of mission. He believed that the philosopher must not waste time on metaphysical abstractions (as, Kant alleged, Wolff and his followers had done). Towards the end of the *Critique of Pure Reason*, Kant described the philosopher as 'not a theorist who occupies himself with conceptions, but a law-giver, legislating for human reason'.[14] Kant saw himself as one such law-giver, offering the world 'a perfectly new science, of which no one has ever even thought . . . and for which nothing hitherto accomplished can be of the smallest use . . .'[15] And what would this science do? Give the faculty of Reason the 'training' it needs; without training, Reason will bear leaves only, without useful fruit.[16]

Indeed, a major purpose behind Kant's studies in epistemology lay in the field of education. In the *Prolegomena to Any Future Metaphysics*, Kant complained that the young wasted their talents pursuing worthless metaphysical questions, such as cosmological proofs of God's existence or speculations about supernatural beings. Kant alleged that these exercises, which he labelled 'dogmatic metaphysics', were only encouraged by the prevailing structure of university studies.[17] The *Critique of Reason*, a critique not of 'books and systems, but of the faculty of reason in general', would provide a new foundation for metaphysics and all other sciences, and regenerate the system of education from its very source: the faculties of the mind.[18]

This concept of critiquing the human faculties with hopes of improving them was, for Kant, the essence, or as he put it, the 'Idea', of education. Kant described what an Idea is and how this concept applies to education in *Pädagogik*, a work published in 1803, shortly before his death. His definition of an Idea as a model of perfection, based not on present experience, but on anticipated perfection, would remain in effect more or less throughout the period discussed in this study, and was a cornerstone of idealist and romantic thought.[19] Kant's application of the term 'Idea' to education would also be reflected in the thought of the next half-century, for it embodied the concepts of *Bildung* and *Erziehung* – building up the mind and drawing forth its faculties – which applied from Fichte to Humboldt, from Coleridge to Newman:

> The idea of an education (*Erziehung*) which develops all man's natural talents is indeed true.[20]

By developing the seeds latent in man in a 'proportional' fashion, the educator could see to it that man, both as an individual and as a race, could achieve his destiny.[21]

Here we encounter the theory that the mind comprises discrete faculties, the development of which makes a human being.[22] Kant examined this process as it took place throughout the student's life. When young, children need mere physical training and discipline.

Like savage nations, children are wild and lack laws to guide them.[23] Man, then, first needs to be disciplined; 'the discipline should not be slavish', however, for 'the child must always feel his freedom'.[24] The trick, then, is to combine the subjugation of the self to laws with a sense of freedom. This paradoxical mixing of force and inner freedom probably owes a good deal to Rousseau's influence. Kant had clearly read *Emile* carefully and admired the French philosopher enormously; indeed, in his small apartment at Königsberg, Kant had only one wall decoration: a portrait of Rousseau.[25] In time, mere discipline should give way to training in basic operations, such as reading and writing. After this, the student must be, according to Kant, 'civilized'; here, Kant is thinking about preparing the student for success in the world. The student must be civilized so that he 'becomes clever, passes in human society, and is beloved and has influence'.[26]

But all this is not enough. A fourth step is needed: man must be made moral. Kant argued that this comes not merely from doing the right, but from obeying maxims for their own sake; or from discovering universally applicable laws for each and every action. This idea of course reflects his thoughts on ethics, worked out in the *Fundamental Principles of the Metaphysics of Morals* (1785) and the *Critique of Practical Reason* (1788). But how is the sense of judgement (*Urteilskraft*) needed for discovering the maxims behind actions to be found? By reason (*Vernunft*). The highest faculty, then, the one that must be developed, is Reason.

Man, said Kant, is neither good nor bad in himself. Kant was still enough of a child of Pietism, though, to believe that, left to his own devices (that is, without reason), man will tend towards evil. Since man is not a moral being by nature, he can become one only if his Reason raises itself up to 'the concepts of duty and laws'.[27] When does man reach this point? When is education finished? Kant was not specific; he did mention, though, that education should last 'until the time that nature itself has determined that people should rule themselves', and that this occurs at about the age of 17.[28] Beyond this point, regular instruction is unnecessary.

Of what use, then, is the university? Kant was not altogether direct in defending his own profession, but he did leave some hints. With adults, instruction leaves the confinements of force and instead stresses the use of a Socratic, dialectical method designed to challenge students to use their reason.[29] And nowhere is this better accomplished than in the study of philosophy, the primary field of the lower faculty. Philosophy is the perfect training for the collegiate mind, for one learns it 'through exercise and independent employment of the reason . . .'[30] But besides providing education for the individual, universities serve the great purpose of educating the entire race, for 'good education is that from which all good in the world springs'.[31] And, said Kant, civilization is at the edge, moving from education aimed at mere disciplining or preparing men for success in society to moral education, education that really subordinates human behaviour and human society to the maxims of pure reason and duty. This type of education originates in the philosophy faculty of the university.

Events late in Kant's life reaffirmed his sense of mission and his profound belief in the primacy of the lower, philosophical faculty. Frederick the Great, long an admirer and promoter of the Enlightenment, died in 1788. His successor, Frederick Wilhelm II, had little taste for enlightened thought and engaged in a futile attempt to extirpate it from his realm and re-establish the primacy of reformed Protestantism. Nowhere was this crackdown stronger than at Königsberg. Two years after ascending to the throne, Frederick Wilhelm dismissed Karl Abraham von Zedlitz from his post as Minister of Cultural and Educational Affairs. Kant had enjoyed a good relationship with von Zedlitz and dedicated his *Critique of Pure Reason* to him. In place of von Zedlitz, the new king appointed Johann Christoph Wöllner, who immediately instituted censorship against free thinking.[32] Candidates in theology at Königsberg were carefully examined for their orthodoxy and warned not to go beyond the limits of their offices as teachers and preachers.[33]

Having spent much of his career assaulting dogmatic concepts of religion, Kant had little stomach for Wöllner. For a time, however, Kant's personal relationship with the King protected him. This protection ceased when Kant published *Religion Within the Limits of Reason Alone* in 1793. The conflict arising out of this book gave Kant an impetus to discuss the role of the lower faculty in the university and that of the university in society.

Before he published *Religion Within the Limits of Reason Alone*, Kant submitted it for approval to the theology faculty at Königsberg. The divines declared that the work was none of their affair since it did not discuss Biblical theology. Kant then sent it to the philosophy faculty at Jena, who gave it their imprimatur. His faith in Jena perhaps reflects the growing reputation of philosophical studies there, which will be discussed later. The book was published on Easter Sunday, 1793.

Kant, like Lessing before him, presents revealed religion as but one part of the larger whole of Reason – a step which, by implication, the human race may outgrow.[34] The essence of religion, said Kant, lies not in divine revelation, but in 'knowledge of our duties as divine commands'.[35] Here, as elsewhere, Reason and Duty stand out as key concepts in Kant's thought.

The imprimatur from Jena, of course, had little force in Prussia; despite it, the work engendered a threatening response from the Prussian state. In October 1794, Wöllner, writing on behalf of the King, informed Kant that 'we expected better of you' and expressed displeasure with Kant's 'irresponsible' behaviour considering his 'duty as teacher of the young'.[36] Wöllner then warned Kant of serious penalties if he persisted in his errors. In his reply, Kant made no effort to be a hero or martyr for the Enlightenment. Instead, he sent the King a carefully worded letter, asserting the right of scholars to debate freely among themselves, yet promising to avoid discussing religious matters in the future.[37] In the mean time, Kant wrote a painstaking analysis of the relationship between the various faculties at a university. He considered it too risky to release while Frederick Wilhelm and Wöllner were in power; after the King died in 1798, however, Kant had the work published as *Der Streit der Fakultäten* [The Struggle of the Faculties].

In this work, Kant argued that the university must enjoy a certain independence, for only the learned can judge the learned.[38] He made a comparison to Adam Smith's economics, stating that universities, like factories, need a division of labour; for that reason, they have traditionally been divided into faculties.[39] Students, moreover, tend to come in two varieties. There are the true scholars (*eigentlichen Gelehrten*) and then there are the careerists, interested only in learning how to get ahead in the civil services. The two groups must be kept apart.

Kant made little effort to disguise his contempt for the careerists, whom he argued the government controls since they will some day deal directly with the '*Idioten*' of the general public.[40] The upper faculties, those of law, medicine and theology, train these budding legalistic bureaucrats. The instructors in these faculties thus themselves fall under government control, for upon taking their posts, they enter into a contractual understanding with the government.[41] The upper faculties are thus tied to their canons and rule-books and must avoid the free employment of Reason. The masses, the '*Idioten*', tend to view members of the upper faculties as magicians dispensing truth. The teachers of law, medicine and theology do little to dispel this unearned honour born out of the laziness of the people themselves. In one mordant passage, Kant attacked the power of the upper faculties, and pointed to the proper check on it:

> The businesspeople of the three upper faculties will always be such magicians if those of the philosophical faculty are not permitted to work publicly against them.[42]

The upper faculties, then, have gained the world, but lost their souls, and have submitted to the government and to laws based on tradition, not Reason. They have become the kept men of knowledge. The only hope for Enlightenment lay in the lower faculty.

Unlike the upper, pre-professional faculties, the lower faculty, said Kant, works in the realm of freedom. It is concerned only with *Wissenschaft*, and may 'hold to its propositions as it sees fit' since it is under 'the law of reason, not that of the government'.[43] And that is why, in Kantian terms, it is free: it may follow the maxims of Reason and subordinate everything to them. This freedom gives the lower faculty the means to check the upper ones; it can 'lay claim to all teachings, in order to put their truth to the test'.[44] The upper faculties may find the objections of the lower troublesome, but they must accept these objections, or else they will become despotic and arrogant.[45]

The lower faculty, through its *Kritik* of the upper, brings the entire university closer to truth. The higher faculties, themselves incapable of pursuing truth freely, are guided down a straighter path along with the civil service and the government.[46] By leading the upper faculties – and giving counsel to the government – the 'lower' faculty, due to its freedom, can be considered the first in importance.[47]

The lower faculty, then, serves as the law-giver of reason. It performs the task for the human race which Kant had outlined a decade earlier in his essay, 'What is Enlightenment?' (1784): gradual enlightenment through the casting off of tutelage in favour of reason. In this work, as in *Der Streit der Fakutäten*, Kant argues that though a person must, as a *Beamter* (civil servant), obey his government, he has an equal duty, as a *Gelehrter*, to pursue reason in complete freedom, and to publish the truths seen thereby for other *Gelehrter* to see. This separation of the 'public' and the 'private' duty almost certainly lay behind the division which Kant saw between the upper and lower faculties. Members of the upper faculties, as 'private' men, as *Beamter*, cannot speak their minds, but the lower faculty, as public *Gelehrter* writing for other scholars, must. What Kant failed to address was that *all* university instructors were *Beamter*, himself included. Despite his protests, Kant himself knuckled under when faced with governmental opposition and gave in to the demands of his prince by refraining from the discussion of religion. Kant, then, presented an *Idea* of how universities should be, but he himself was unable always to act in accordance with it.

Kant's words, then, were to provide a philosophical framework for the romantic Idea of a university. But another source would tie these ideas into the broad cultural underpinnings of Romanticism. This element was the neo-humanism which arose at Weimar under the careful guidance of Wolfgang Goethe, Germany's greatest man of letters. New ideas about civilization and the means to cultivate it arose in this tiny ducal capital. The Duke of Weimar, moreover, retained primary control over the University of Jena.

One reason a ducal court could have such cultural importance was the remarkable political decentralization of Germany. Most German states of the eighteenth century were ruled by princes who enjoyed near complete autonomy within the Germany empire. Princes were as enlightened or obscurantist as they wished in their petty despotisms, for the empire had relinquished any real control over local affairs centuries earlier. The freedom princes enjoyed could be a bane or a blessing. Most German princes tyrannized their realms, yet the tutor of one under-aged German duke compared the situation to the flower of antiquity and wrote:

> The German nation is not really a nation, but an aggregate of many nations, like ancient Greece.[48]

This tutor, C. M. Wieland, had a special reason for optimism. His charge would soon come of age, and as Karl August, Duke of Weimar, would rule over a court famed throughout Germany for its letters.

But Wieland did not stay on as tutor after Karl August, in 1775, reached his maturity. Tired of domination by his mother and his teacher, the young Duke dismissed Wieland from his teaching duties but allowed him to remain at court. In his place, the Duke brought in a young attorney and literary man named Wolfgang von Goethe, who had recently made quite a sensation with his tragic novel, *The Sorrows of Young Werther*.[49] Goethe remained at Weimar until his death in 1831.

In time, Goethe became more famous than his ducal patron. There was, according to W. H. Bruford, an underlying purpose behind his humanistic activity. Goethe, says Bruford, came to view developing his own creative faculties – and those of others – as a mission of paramount importance. Goethe even went so far as to leave Weimar for two years (as described in his *Italian Journey*) to develop his appreciation for the beautiful by studying botany. Upon his return, Goethe continued to work with the idea of *'allgemeine Bildung'* – general education – of the human person.

But what form would this education take? Goethe was not a professional educator, a university professor or a private tutor. To Goethe, *Bildung* came not through a set curriculum or even institutions, but by encountering things and people in the world and interacting with them.[50]

Goethe described this process in his episodic novel *Wilhelm Meister's Apprenticeship* (published in instalments, 1778–96). Wilhelm, son of a businessman, goes out with a troupe of travelling actors, encountering all sorts of people on the way. Like Rousseau's Emile, Wilhelm learns through experience. But there is no tutor: the experiences are encountered freely and are not carefully engineered to protect the young soul from the wrong influences. Instead, art, life and people shape Wilhelm, much as they shaped Goethe himself.[51] As Wilhelm notes in Book V of the *Apprenticeship*,

> To speak it in a word; the cultivation of my individual self, here as I am, has from my youth upwards been constantly though dimly my wish and my purpose.[52]

Goethe did not theorize about higher education in particular, but did provide an ideal for it to meet. This was the ideal of *Bildung*, of free cultivation and development of the faculties. Moreover, though he was not himself at the University of Jena, Goethe's important position at Weimar would help put Jena on the academic map of Germany. As an informal culture minister for the Duke, Goethe wielded great influence over appointments at Jena. His name would draw important people to the university and his influence could protect them from harm. One of the first major appointments to Jena engineered by Goethe was that of Friedrich Schiller.

Given his humble origins, one might not expect Schiller to play the role in German cultural life which he did. He was born in 1759 in the dukedom of Würtemburg to an army surgeon (then considered little more socially than a barber). It was here, in his own province, that Schiller came face to face with the worst aspects of life in tiny German states. As a boy Schiller longed to become a clergyman. Karl Eugene, the Duke of Würtemburg, had other plans. In a prime example of paternalistic interference, the Duke ordered Schiller sent to a secular school, thus closing Schiller out of a clerical career. The Duke, moreover, made plans for Schiller's higher education. Even though the University of Tübingen stood nearby, the Duke established a military academy of his own which stressed martial discipline and offered little in the way of an education in the humanities. Karl Eugene pressured Schiller into this school in 1773.

To Schiller, this place was little more than a prison camp. The Duke forced him into the study of law (which Schiller loathed); and later he switched to the medical faculty. These studies all took a secondary position to Schiller's interest in poetry and drama. Schiller, in fact, led a double life as a student. He studied law and medicine, but kept carefully hidden manuscripts of poems and plays, which he wrote in secret.[53] Even after leaving this academic prison with a degree in medicine, Schiller was still under the Duke's control. He was assigned as a doctor to a rag-tag regiment composed of the dregs of German society. Yet the stage called: he finished his first play (*The Robbers*) and sneaked out of the Dukedom to Mannheim to see his play performed.

The play was a success – but not with the Duke. Karl Eugene eventually detained Schiller and forbad him to publish anything except medical texts.[54] This infringement on his freedom was, for Schiller, the last straw. After careful arrangements, Schiller left his home duchy for good.

Schiller saw how restrictive and limited life could be in these tiny Germany states. But Germany was not without its blessings. If one could not get along with the local despot, one could always escape to a nearby duchy or free city. A growing interest in theatre, spurred on by travelling troupes, offered a creative outlet. German princes could use their powers for the furtherance of the arts and academic life; indeed, no one was more unlike Karl Eugene of Württemburg than Karl August of Weimar. Schiller had the good fortune to meet the latter prince in 1784. The Duke, recognizing Schiller as a rising talent, gave him a title – and with it, an attachment to a new German state.[55] Three years later, Schiller moved to Weimar.

During the same year in which he met Karl August, Schiller gave a lecture at the Germany Society of the Palatinate which set out his feelings about universities. In this work, entitled 'Was kann eine gute stehende Schaubuhne eigentlich wirken' (What Good Can a Standing Theatre Really Do?), Schiller attacked the universities and argued that theatre can do the job of educating the nation better than they. While there were 'great, learned people, who broaden the horizons of human knowledge', at universities, there were also 'dumb pedants, who guard their quarto volumes'.[56] Schiller was deeply annoyed at the philistine atmosphere of Germany's petty despotisms and vented his pent-up rage from his years at the academy in Würtemberg:

> Does one condemn the young man, who, driven by inner power, steps out of the narrow prison of vocational studies and follows the call of God which lies within himself? . . . Is this the revenge of small minds against the genius, whom they despair of following upwards?[57]

Here spoke the brilliant dramatist who remembered virtual enslavement to legal and medical studies while his school ignored his real calling.

In contrast to the sterile pedantry of school, the theatre, argued Schiller, offers an education which develops the whole person. Schiller praised it, saying:

> The stage is the establishment where enjoyment joins with instruction, rest with exertion, and amusement with education; where no power of the soul is flexed to the disadvantage of another . . .[58]

The theatre, then, should be supported by princes, for it can develop aesthetic judgement in their subjects.[59] It can make their subject moral; it revives the self-satisfied businessman, the pedantic scholar and the low-living commoner.[60] The theatre is the vehicle for state education, not the university.

But fate decreed that Schiller would have a role in university as well as in theatrical life. His work in both areas would come at the behest of Karl August of Weimar. After several years of eking out a living, Schiller decided to seek out the Duke and Goethe in 1787. When Schiller first arrived at Weimar, both these famous men were out of town. Schiller made the best of an unpromising situation and talked to the remaining luminaries in this small but cultured city. These included Johann Gottfried von Herder (the court chaplain whose ideas about culture were a foundation for historicism) and the famous poet Christoph Martin Wieland, the Duke's old tutor. Shortly after meeting these men, Schiller went to nearby Jena and met Karl Leonhard Reinhold, a professor of philosophy at Jena and a fierce Kantian. Reinhold, who was Wieland's son-in-law, mentioned that it might be easy to find a chair at Jena for Schiller.[61]

But a chair in what? Reinhold's offer seems to indicate how informal faculty selection was in the eighteenth century. One met a few influential people (preferably people with access to the local duke or elector) and found a chair. Schiller had no teaching experience at all, and no degree except one in medicine from the military academy in Stuttgart. But he was getting to know the right people. Talk of a chair motivated him to leave drama behind for a time and encouraged him to finish his first historical work, *The History of the Secession of the United Netherlands from Spanish Rule*. This work was well received and quickly gave Schiller a reputation as a popular historian. Late in 1788, a chair opened up at Jena, and on Goethe's advice, the Duke approved Schiller's appointment to it.

Before his history of the Dutch Revolt, Schiller had no experience as an historian. The university quickly gave him a degree to make up for his lack of any real professional credentials.[62] And Schiller almost did not accept the appointment, for the 200 thaler per annum that came with it could not possibly support himself and his intended bride, Charlotte. Only after the Duke and Charlotte's family each agreed to give the young couple 200 thalers a year in addition to the stipend from the chair did Schiller accept the post.[63] The age of the highly paid German professor had yet to come. Through Schiller, though, Weimar humanism would gain a foothold at Jena.

Jena, in 1789, seemed similar to other German universities. Like the others, it was controlled by local German authorities. Although the Duke of Weimar held the pre-eminent position (and contributed the most money), the Duke shared his authority with the courts of Meiningen, Gotha and Coburg. These courts often opposed Karl August's efforts to reshape the university and sometimes presented alternatives to his candidates for chairs.[64] The Duke *de facto* deferred control of the university to Goethe and Christian Gottlob Voigt, another of his privy councillors.[65] The town of Jena contained about 4,000 inhabitants; the university, about 1,000 students. Students once came from many parts of Germany, but local restrictions on foreign study (which became more common in the middle of the century) cut sharply into the number of students from other German states.[66] Teaching was done in much the same way as elsewhere. Professors were required to give public lectures (for their salaries), but many also offered private ones, paid for directly by students. The medieval practice of the disputation survived; the seminar was yet to come.[67] Professors – as shown by Schiller's salary – were not well paid. Many tried to make ends meet by other means, including the sale of alcohol.[68] Most students preferred the vocational studies, or *Brotstudium*, of law, medicine and theology to studies in the philosophy faculty. They were there not for a general education, but to prepare themselves for lucrative careers. They drank, caroused, carried swords and duelled much as German students did everywhere.

But Jena was entering into a new era, a brief time when it would play a greater role than ever in the history of higher education. Kantian philosophy, Goethe and Voigt attracted great scholars such as Fichte, who in turn brought in more and better students.[69] 'The French Revolution,' wrote Friedrich Schlegel, 'Fichte's *Wissenschaftslehre* and Goethe's *Meister* are the greatest trends of the age', and all of these would come together at Jena.[70]

The goals of Weimar humanism, of Goethe, became Schiller's as well. Schiller brought these ideas about education with him when he came to Jena. The old dislike of empty pedantry remained; so too did the farseeing goal of a better cultivated human race. For a time, Schiller accepted the university as a place where this education could take place. But he did so not without complaints and reservations, and nowhere is this more evident than in his first public lecture at Jena, 'What is and to what end does one study universal history?', delivered in May 1789.

One should not be deceived by the title: this work is mostly about studying, not history. Schiller expressed profound dissatisfaction with the type of study then prevalent at German universities. He freely acknowledged that all people have different callings in the world. But all have one calling in common: 'to educate themselves as human beings.'[71] This is a great and noble calling, one which, Schiller argued, the study of history was tailor-made to fulfil.

But many students fail in this calling. They study only what they need for their careers, ignoring that which 'the spirit only as spirit enjoys'.[72] Such '*Brodgelehrten*' (*sic*; literally, 'bread-learned') servants of the body instead of the spirit resist all efforts to reform universities, since such reform would mean more work. To the *Brodgelehrten*, seeking truth would be a vain activity, for 'he does not exchange truth for gold, for the praise of gazettes, for the favour of princes'.[73] Though these careerists live in a world of 'complete freedom', they carry around a slave's soul.

The situation is even worse for the truly gifted student. He finds himself in a confining, frustrating environment which forces him on to a prescribed career path regardless of his gifts. As a result, says Schiller, 'his genius will rebel against his vocation'.[74] The narrowness of his surroundings drives him to the ground; as a result, many a gifted attorney, doctor or minister leaves his office in disgust. All of this, of course, seems autobiographical: who more than Schiller himself, with his wretched school experience and subsequent devotion to letters (instead of medicine) better exemplified this situation?

Yet there is more to this scenario than Schiller's complaints about his own troubled youth. One cannot help but notice a sharp distinction between flesh and spirit in Schiller's lectures. The students whom he attacked are literally the 'bread-learned' (*Brodgelehrten*). They are tied to the world of the flesh; of money, prestige and petty courts. None the less, there remains, besides the grovelling materialist and the frustrated genius, the 'philosophical head' (*philosophisches Kopf*). These are the servants of the spirit and stand in direct opposition to everything the empty careerist represents. Instead of picking a course of study designed only to meet his narrow interests, the philosophical head seeks breadth, for 'where the vocationalist divides, the philosophical spirit unites'.[75] The philosophical head welcomes new ideas, new curricula and good intellectual company. And he alone has the capacity to study the subject which was the purported topic of Schiller's lecture: world history.

The philosophical head alone can benefit from the wonders of the human past. He can assimilate the occurrences of all ages, and go beyond mere events to an understanding of history as a whole, with all its moral lessons. History becomes an expression of spirit which can only be comprehended by the philosophically-oriented student.

Schiller's turn to teaching history in an academic setting did not represent as radical a departure from the stage as one might think. Towards the end of the 1789 lecture on world history, Schiller presented the human past as a stage:

> A person is changed and flees from the stage; his beliefs flee and
> are changed with him: history alone remains uninterrupted on
> the stage, an immortal inhabitant of all nations and times.[76]

Since Schiller viewed history as an enormous stage, he advocated
its use as a tool for education for the same reason he wanted to
use theatre: the education of man, both individually and collec-
tively. Schiller outlined the role of aesthetics in education in several
works dating from the mid-1790s, the most famous of which was
his series of letters published as *The Aesthetic Education of Man*.

Schiller's thoughts on education formed a remarkably coherent
whole. He sharply distinguished between the flesh and the spirit,
strongly favouring the latter. The world of the flesh was that of his
hated military academy, or of the narrow-minded *Brodgelehrten*. But
in the realm of the spirit, of the philosophical head, of world history,
true freedom reigned. Even when he started teaching world history,
Schiller never stopped thinking as a dramatist; to him, all the world
was quite literally a stage. This stage developed the human soul by
presenting conflicts between man and nature, man and society, man
and himself.

The university nevertheless proved to be too small a stage for
him. He got a taste of pedantic silliness soon after arriving at Jena.
In the autumn of 1789, he published his inaugural lecture on world
history (discussed above) with the subtitle 'by Friedrich Schiller,
Professor of History in Jena'. Schiller was technically not a professor of history, but one of philosophy – and an adjunct one at
that. The resident professor of history vehemently objected to Schiller's
use of this title. Schiller used it in innocence and considered the
fighting over titles silly. He wound up having little to do with his
academic colleagues during his stay at Jena.[77]

Schiller's health failed after 1791 and he spent most of his life
thereafter confined to his home. He completed another major historical work, *The History of the Thirty Years' War* (1792) along with
some major works in aesthetics, including *The Aesthetic Education
of Man* (1795) and *On Naive and Sentimental Poetry* (1796). As the
1790s wore on, Schiller lost interest in historical writing and the
university. He longed to return to drama and moved back to Weimar
in 1799. After writing several of his best plays (including *Wallenstein*,
*Mary Stuart* and others based on historical personages) he died in
1805, after almost fifteen years of ill health.

Schiller was only a sojourner in academe, not a permanent resident. Through him, though, the Weimar ideal of self-cultivation entered the university environment. Schiller did not have the strength or inclination to carry these ideas into the realm of academic politics. This task fell to a contemporary of his at Jena, Johann Gottlieb Fichte.

While Schiller merely visited the academic world, Fichte made the university and intellectual life the core of his being. Though the son of a poor Saxon linen weaver, Fichte managed to obtain a good education through the benevolent support of a local baron. He went to the Pforta school, one of the best secondary schools in Germany, and then studied theology at Jena (*c.* 1780), Wittemberg and Leipzig. Financial difficulties forced him to interrupt his studies and take on work as a private tutor. His independence, wilfulness and quick temper got him into frequent disputes with his employers; he detested being a tutor. As would often be the case in the future, his teaching duties shaped his research. Some of Fichte's students wanted to learn about the new ideas of Immanuel Kant. In order to instruct them better, Fichte engaged in a close study of Kant's three critiques.

Much as Luther's life was changed through the study of St. Paul's epistles, so was Fichte's entire outlook restructured by reading Kant. Kant's books persuaded Fichte to leave behind the determinism of his youth (derived from Wolff) and made him the staunch advocate of free will, dignity and duty which he was for the rest of his life. By 1791, Fichte wanted nothing more than to meet the sage of Königsberg and to gain his support. He managed to meet Kant in 1791, but Kant was cool to him. So Fichte wrote a philosophical work designed to gain Kant's attention: *An Attempt at a Critique of All Revelation*. Much like Kant's own *Religion within the Limits of Reason Alone*, Fichte's work applied critical philosophy to the religious world. Kant was so impressed by this that he met Fichte again, found a publisher for the work and arranged for Fichte to get a new tutoring position. Published anonymously, Fichte's *Critique* found an appreciative audience among Kantians, most of whom thought Kant himself had written it. Kant eventually revealed the author's true identity, thereby making Fichte famous almost overnight.

Fichte's new association with Kant opened the door for his arrival at Jena. R. L. Reinhold, a professor of philosophy, made Jena a centre of Kantian ideas. Reinhold vacated his chair in 1794 to accept a position at Kiel. It was decided to dedicate this adjunct chair in philosophy to the spread of Kant's critical philosophy.[78] Fichte's fame from the *Critique of all Revelations* brought him to the attention of Goethe; with the support of Goethe and Duke Karl August, Fichte obtained the chair and began teaching in the summer of 1794.

One wonders if Goethe knew what kind of firebrand Fichte was. The new professor has often been called a Jacobin. This may be an overstatement, but he was certainly a proponent of radical change. In 1793, he published a pamphlet entitled 'Recovery of Freedom of Thought from European Princes' which vehemently attacked limits on freedom of thought. The work appeared anonymously and was said to come from 'Heliopolis, in the last year of the old darkness'.[79] Fichte shared in the Jacobin dream that the end of darkness had come; it seems hardly a coincidence that the last year of the old darkness was also the first of the French Republic. But Fichte argued for gradual enlightenment, much as Kant did. To Fichte, this enlightenment would come about through the free exchange of ideas which was then blocked by princes who served obscurantist folly.

In reforming the world, though, Fichte wanted to start at the university. Upon arriving at Jena, Fichte immediately set to work changing the institution. His first official act was a series of public lectures, held on Friday evenings, on 'The Scholar's Vocation'.[80] Fichte regularly packed the largest lecture hall in town (which held 500 people) with attentive listeners. The crowds were not disappointed. These lectures present a remarkably coherent and all-embracing discussion of the moral purpose of the scholar.

The first lecture began with a paean to the dignity of man. Fichte presented the concept of the 'self-positing I' which formed the bases of his later *Wissenschaftslehre* (Science of Knowledge). Man – the 'I' has a final end: 'to subordinate to himself all that is irrational, to master it freely and according to his own laws.'[81] But since this goal is not attainable, man's real vocation is ceaseless striving towards this goal. Scholars, including Fichte himself, have a special role in this process.

Fichte had a grandiose, almost messianic view of the scholar's importance. He charged his students to 'pass on that education which you have received and on very side to raise our fellowmen to a higher level of culture'.[82] The learned elite would lead the way in introducing the new world. Universities and scholars were thus the means for the moral regeneration of mankind.

In the third lecture, Fichte reached sublime heights when considering the scholar's vocation. The scholar could boast:

> my existence has no limit. I am eternal . . . I lift my head boldly
> to the threatening stony heights, to the roaring cataracts, and
> to the crashing clouds in their fire-red sea. 'I am eternal' I shout to
> them. 'I defy your power. . . . For I have found my vocation, and
> it is more permanent than you. It is eternal, and so too am I.'[83]

Fichte here chose stock, natural images of the sublime poets, and, like Shelley and Wordsworth, presented the mind of man as greater than the nature around it. Man – and especially the scholar – can look all the forces of nature in the face and overcome them due to the endless capacity to develop his own consciousness and that of humanity. Fichte's scholar is not unlike Wordsworth's vision of the self presented in the tenth book of *The Prelude*:

> When I began at first, in early youth
> To yield myself to Nature – when that strong
> And holy passion overcame me first –
> Neither day nor night, evening or morn,
> Were free from the oppression, but, great God,
> Who send'st thyself into this breathing world
> through Nature and through every kind of life,
> and mak'st man what he is, creature divine,
> In single or in social eminence,
> Above all these raised infinite ascents
> When reason, which enables him to be,
> Is not sequestered – what a change is here!
>
> Bk. X, ll. 381–92

To Fichte, as well as to Wordsworth and other Romantics, the mind of man towers above the threatening forces of nature. And Fichte would certainly agree that this divinity applies to man 'in single or social eminence', to man in society as well as man the individual.

Scholars, then, promote 'the equal, continuous, and progressive development of all human talents'; not only his own, but those of society at large.[84] They aim for the 'ethical improvement of the whole person', forming a special class which provides, by its own self-development, an excellent example for others. Fichte compared them to the disciples of Christ, referring to Matthew 5:13 ('you are the salt of the earth'). Indeed, he finally called himself a 'priest of truth'.[85] All this squares very well with the ideas presented by Kant in *The Conflict of the Faculties*, for Kant also envisaged a learned class (the philosophical faculty) who would act as intellectual law-givers for society. In Coleridge's hands, this class would become the Christian clerisy. But Kant expressed his ideas in a book which he published late in his career, and only after Wilhelm II died. Nowhere did he make so open and strident a statement as the young Fichte did in his inaugural lectures.

Fichte also shared Kant's wish to revolutionize the world of phil-osophy and make philosophical studies the foundation for all knowledge. He took the subjective concepts of Kant's epistemology (as Kant discussed them in the *Critique of Pure Reason*) and expressed them in a sharp and even belligerent way. In 1794, Fichte wrote that 'Philosophy teaches us to seek everything within the I.' The I, the '*Ich*' or self, is the centre of all creation; for 'human observa-tion holds together the planets . . . thanks to it, the suns move in their allotted path. From the lichen to the seraphim, this immense hierarchy owe its existence to the I.'[86] This concept of the 'self-positing I' served as the foundation for Fichte's most famous work, the *Wissenschaftslehre* (The Science of Knowledge).

With this study, Fichte claimed to be completing the philosophi-cal work of Kant. The *Wissenschaftslehre* would be the foundation of all future human knowledge, the 'science of science as such'.[87] Fichte worked in the tradition of Kant's Copernican revolution in philosophy, placing the knowing mind – rather than the material object – at the centre:

> The object shall be posited and determined by the cognitive fac-ulty, and not the cognitive faculty by the subject.[88]

Fichte spoke disparagingly of all 'dogmatism' and 'materialism' which presented a simplistic empiricism. He thus broke with the episte-mological foundations of the Enlightenment, further clearing the way for the subjectivity of the Romantic Age. Though he (like Kant) spoke constantly of the laws of reason, he none the less argued that one's personality type, as much as one's reason, would deter-mine what kind of philosophy one espouses:

> A philosophical system is not a dead piece of furniture that we can reject or accept as we wish; it is rather a thing animated by the soul of the person who holds it.[89]

A person, then, takes on a philosophy which corresponds to his character. The weak cave in to materialism or dogmatism, while the strong see the merits and enjoy the freedoms of idealistic philosophy. After all, Idealism comes not from a passive acceptance of the world, but an active placement of the self in it:

> The self's own positing of itself is thus its own pure activity. The *self posits itself*, and by virtue of this mere self-assertion it *exists.*[90]

Fichte's philosophy is thus a philosophy of *action*. It suited his aggressive, belligerent personality perfectly. Nowhere did Fichte *act* more than as a teacher.

Indeed, the whole reason Fichte wrote his *Wissenschaftslehre* down grew out of his teaching. In the opening to his *First Introduction to the Wissenschaftslehre* (1797), Fichte observed that

> In pursuit of my academic duties I at first wrote for my students in the classroom, where I had it in my power to continue with my verbal explanations until I was understood.[91]

Manuscripts of the *Wissenschaftslehre* – designed as teaching aids – began floating around (perhaps in incomplete form); since some misinterpreted them, Fichte published his ideas in print form and continuously revised them. But lectures, and teaching, always came first.

Judging from contemporary accounts, studying under Fichte was a frightening but worthwhile experience – which was what Fichte wanted. One student called him 'the Bonaparte of philosophy'; another noted that

> The demands which Fichte makes upon his students are so great that at first we almost lost all of our courage.[92]

Fichte intentionally presented himself as a force to be reckoned with. He held lectures at special times – Friday afternoons, Sundays after church, early morning – all designed to draw audiences and achieve an impact. Before his lectures at seven in the morning he would go riding and arrive at the lecture hall with his riding crop and his bravado. He constantly attacked those who merely crammed; one member of the audience noted that 'not a class goes by in which he does not warn us against regurgitation and an empty philosophy of words'.[93] A *Privatdozent* at Jena wrote that Fichte was 'like a thunderstorm', and that Fichte

> does not move the soul, like Reinhold, but uplifts it. The former (Reinhold) sought to make good men; the latter wishes to make great ones.[94]

Fichte's eyes, the *Dozent*, continues, were 'punishing'; his swagger 'defiant'.[95] But Fichte's aim was clear: to engage the student, foster his moral and intellectual development, and make him worthy of the study of philosophy. Fichte was the sublime educator, a powerful human will who, like the mighty forces of nature, built up the souls of his students by inspiring fear, awe and wonder.

Fichte did more for his students than just give overpowering lectures, for his moral vision for the university extended beyond his lecture hall. Towards the end of his first year at Jena (1794–5), Fichte engaged in a headlong assault on the wretched duelling fraternities. To him, they were a dreadful waste, encouraging drunkenness and violence instead of scholarship. He urged that the university disband them entirely. Nothing of the sort happened; most other faculty members felt intimidated by them (not without reason) and did not join the reform efforts of this young upstart in the philosophy faculty. Thugs from the fraternities physically attacked Fichte's house, throwing rocks through its windows and frightening his family. Fichte was so incensed that he cancelled his summer 1795 lectures, left town and informed Karl August that he would not return unless the Duke arrested the ringleaders of the fraternities and guaranteed the safety of Fichte's family. The students rioted after Fichte left, and the army was called in to quell them. When peace was restored, Fichte returned in time to teach in the autumn.

But things were not the same. For all his moral courage, Fichte had failed to eradicate the menace of the fraternities. He abandoned reshaping the entire university. Instead, he would now work on enlarging the souls of those students who would follow him voluntarily. Fichte wrote:

> Around the higher man others form a circle, in which those with the greatest humanity are nearest the center.[96]

It was these students, those with the 'greatest humanity', whom Fichte now tried to serve. Cancelling his public lectures, Fichte continued private lectures and teaching. He held informal meetings, called 'conservatoria' with philosophy students, where they could ask questions and raise objections to his ideas.[97] For new students, he developed the first real introductory course in philosophy; for advanced scholars, he offered a chance to publish in a philosophical journal that he edited. In all, he aimed to shake university studies out of the somnabulance and vocationalism which plagued them through the eighteenth century, and instead wanted universities to be the font of ideas for a new world order. In Fichte's philosophy, the self posited itself by the *Act*; and Fichte himself strove to live up to this dictum.

But all this activity would come to nothing if there were no response from students. As Rudolf Lassahn points out, Fichte did not found a specific philosophical school of thought. In Fichte's day there were Kantians; in the next generation, there were self-professed Hegelians of every stripe. But no one called himself a 'Fichtean'.[98] Instead, there were students influenced by Fichte who went on to promote some of his ideas without becoming disciples. Indeed, Fichte himself would probably abhor sycophantic followers, for the First Introduction to the *Wissenschaftslehre* begins:

> Attend to yourself: turn your attention away from everything that surrounds you and towards your inner life; this is the first demand that philosophy makes of its disciple.[99]

Fichte wanted his students to think and act for themselves and obey their own inner law; he wanted them to become disciples of *philosophy*, not of their teacher.

Soon after Fichte's arrival at Jena, a group of his students formed a society to discuss his ideas. This *Literarische Gesellschaft* (Literary Society) was small; about 45 young men in total joined between 1794 and 1799.[100] Historians have recovered the constitution and protocol book of this group. Members called themselves 'free men', refusing to claim allegiance to anything like a fraternity. Rather than duelling and drinking, the organization fostered study and knowledge, for its constitution forbade 'all undertakings which do not contribute to the education of the head and heart'.[101] As with Fichte, education and its benefits for society headed their agenda. They discussed Fichte's lectures on 'The Scholar's Vocation', as well as Goethe's *Wilhelm Meister*. The Free Men were generally republicans, and dreamed of a republican and democratic state which rested on the kind of education they promoted. Some members went on to become educators themselves at both the secondary and university levels.

But the most famous group associated with Fichte was the Jena romantic school. Fichte was one of the catalysts which brought this school into existence. One by one, great poets and writers came to Jena – in part because of its proximity to Weimar and Goethe, in part because of Schiller, but also because of the growing fame of Fichte. The poet Höderlin, came in November 1794, and heard Fichte almost every day.[102] From a careful study of the *Wissenschaftslehre* he developed an interest in popular education. The Schlegel brothers arrived in 1796, while Schelling came two years later to a post which Fichte prepared for him.[103] Most of these men, along with Tieck, heard Fichte's lectures and attended his *convervatoria*. Fichte was, as Lassahn puts it, their 'spiritual centre'. His new philosophy of the *Ich* and his energetic style appealed to a new generation which stressed individual thought and subjectivity. Bear in mind, though: Fichte was not speaking of the *Ich* as unbridled individualism. Quite the contrary: Fichte's idea of the true self was he who knew the inner laws of reason and realized his obligations to society. In later years, Fichte would publish a work hostile to Tieck and other Romantics.[104] His influence on them none the less remains undeniable. It was he who introduced them to Kant, to the new subjective epistemology, and the heightened sense of the powers of the human mind to master the world. His personal powers may have overwhelmed them at Jena, but the very fact that he later disagreed with them (much as he himself was eventually rejected by Kant) shows that he was a successful teacher. He did not create mindless disciples, but helped the finest generation of German poets come into a mastery of their own supreme faculties. Goethe reflected on Jena at this time, writing:

> The University at Jena stood at the peak of its glory; the combined effect of talented persons and fortunate circumstances would merit the most accurate and vivid description.[105]

For all his talents as a teacher, though, Fichte never won the support of his colleagues. After all, he was not an ordinary (resident) professor, but a extraordinary (adjunct) one. Colleagues objected to his holding lectures on Sunday and called it a violation of the Sabbath. None came to his aid during his fight with the fraternities. His leftist politics and sympathy for the revolution in France aroused suspicion among older, ordinary professors, especially those in the theology faculty. Fichte's last battle at Jena would be with this 'upper' faculty; this conflict would in some respects be a repetition of Kant's struggle at Königsberg, but due largely to Fichte's personality, the final outcome would be very different.

As in Kant's case, the fracas began with a member of the philosophy faculty having the audacity to discuss religion. Late in 1798, Fichte published 'Über der Grund unseres Glaubens an eine göttliche Weltregierung' (On the Basis for our Belief in a Divine World Order). In this work, Fichte attempted to include religion within the framework of his *Wissehschaftslehre*, much as Kant had tried to discuss religion within the limits of pure reason. Some people in anonymous publications accused Fichte of atheism. Fichte was no atheist (for that matter, neither was Kant), but his political radicalism and belligerent personality made him a target for the theology faculty. Pamphlets flew back and forth between Fichte (and his supporters) and Fichte's enemies.

Unlike Kant's dispute with the King of Prussia, this affair was noisy, ugly and very public. Fichte, moreover, refused to accept any correction from the government. He complained in a letter to Reinhold: 'Kant's luck was his obscurity'; but Fichte's aggressive style ensured he would be the centre of attention.[106] Formal charges of atheism were made to electoral Saxony, which shared jurisdiction over Jena with the Duke of Weimar. But Fichte refused to accept any censure or to recognize the right of a political ruler to tell him what to write. Unlike Kant, he was the stuff that martyrs are made of: pride, self-righteousness, tactlessness and complete dedication to the cause of academic freedom. Goethe, who had stood by him during his fight with the fraternities, did not do so now. The last straw came in March 1799, when Fichte wrote to a privy councillor in Weimar, swearing that if censured by the Duke, he would resign and, with his loyal supporters, found a new university. This temerity was too much for Goethe and Karl August. The Duke accepted his resignation; Fichte thus lost his post and left for Berlin in June 1799.

The subsequent history of Jena perhaps lends some credence to Fichte's inflated sense of his own importance. New inscriptions of students dropped significantly – from 382 in 1798 to 225 only two years later. Personal disputes broke out between the Schlegel brothers and Schiller (over ideas) and August Schlegel and Schelling (over

Caroline Schlegel). The Jena romantic school, formed largely under Fichte's influence, did not long survive his tenure there. Tieck and the Schlegels left; Novalis died; Schelling married August Schlegel's former wife and moved to Berlin. Even before Napoleon's victory at Jena in 1806, the university had passed its peak.

Fichte none the less left a legacy which outlived Jena's height. He gave Jena – and, really, all subsequent German universities – a new Idea, a new *raison d'être*: the education of men and of man. Individuals came to have their rational and moral faculties challenged and enlarged; they, in turn, would take their heightened philosophical and moral sensitivities to the world around them. Mere preparation for ministry, law or medicine was no longer nearly enough, Fichte, then, represented the coming victory of the philosophical faculty over the so-called 'upper faculties', for it was the philosophical faculty which now caught the attention of students. And Fichte, above all, represented the struggle for academic freedom, for the scholar to be subject not to earthly powers, but the call of the *Ich*, the metaphysical self, within him. Fichte would rather lose his job than submit to a prince; this was his greatest revenge on the careerism of the past.

Fichte took the idea of *Bildung* promoted by Goethe and gave it a place in the academic setting. To do so, he employed Kant's idealistic philosophy, tying the goals of education to the new epistemology and moral theory of the Sage of Königsberg. He offered a solution to the basic question of *why* one studies at a university: to develop one's own mind and the collective *Ich* of society at large. But *what* would be studied? Granted, Fichte was an active educator and a proponent of the study of philosophy. Like Kant before him, he stood for the new, expanded role of the philosophy faculty in the university system. But the philosophy faculty, in fact, included all studies which did not directly lead to the legal, medical or clerical professions. Languages, history, physical and biological science, geography, mathematics and related fields all fell within its scope. What of these studies? Did they, like metaphysics and ethics, have a new place in the academic world?

It is here that another element discussed at the beginning at this chapter comes into play. As noted above, classical studies had, under Heyne, experienced a revival in German academe. Doubtless the fascination with ancient Greece exhibited by Winkelmann and Lessing also contributed to the new interest in antiquity.[107] One of Heyne's students, A. W. Schlegel, brought the new interest in the ancient world to Jena.

The son of a Hanoverian official, August Wilhelm Schlegel (b. 1767) went to Göttingen in 1786 to study theology. But he switched faculties, entering the philosophy faculty to study classics. Here, he participated in Heyne's revolutionary new type of class – the seminar. Heyne's seminar was in philology. Schlegel later became an admirer of Herder, applying Herder's ideas about culture to Dante's *Commedia*.[108] By the mid-1790s, he had come to the attention of Friedrich Schiller, who was about to start publishing a literary journal, *Die Horen* (The Graces). Schiller wanted an assistant for this project, and also believed a philologist and literary historian would come in handy at Jena.[109] So A. W. Schlegel came to the city in 1796, and married Caroline Michaelis, daughter of a famed professor at Göttingen.

Under Schiller's tutelage, between 1796 and 1800 August Schlegel published some 300 reviews of contemporary literature.[110] He also served briefly as an adjunct professor in the philosophy faculty. He had little new to say on education or philosophy, for he worked mainly to spread the ideas of Goethe and Schiller. But his interest in classical antiquity was shared by his younger brother Friedrich; and a more unlike pair of brothers has perhaps never existed.

Brash, bold and given to violent passions, Friedrich Schlegel embodied the temperament which today one would typically call 'romantic'. Five years younger than August, Friedrich was sent by his parents to join his brother at Göttingen when he was 17. During the early 1790s, he went to Leipzig, exhausted his financial resources, lived off his brother and contemplated suicide.[111] He wrote to his brother in 1793:

> I can no longer be fettered – I must and will by myself live, confident and unconcerned about what I encounter.[112]

Struggle and inner division characterized his life and his outlook. Leaping from exaltation to despair and back again, he was raw talent, undisciplined brilliance incarnate. Like Goethe and many Germans in his own generation, Schlegel was enamoured of Shakespeare; borrowing a motif from *Hamlet*, Schlegel wrote of his own existence:

> Humanity is marvellously beautiful, endlessly rich – and the feeling of our grace consumes each moment of my life. And then there are times, when the best which I think of myself, my virtue, even if it were at that moment achievable, sickens me.[113]

Such a passionate, brilliant young man needed a passionate, brilliant teacher to help give some form and balance to his unevenly developed faculties.

When Friedrich Schlegel joined his brother in Jena in 1796, he found this teacher: Johann Gottlieb Fichte. August admired Fichte and attended his lectures. But Friedrich became fascinated with him, finding in his teachings the core around which to develop his own ideas (much as Fichte himself had with Kant). Fichte's talk of the self-positing *Ich* making itself exist through its actions appealed to the egocentric young man. Fichte's aggressive, theatrical teaching style doubtlessly also had its charms for Friedrich.

Friedrich Schlegel nevertheless could not be a mere disciple. He used Fichte's ideas in new ways, integrating them into his emotional nature and his interests in antiquity. For unlike Fichte, Schlegel was no rationalist. The unfeeling logic of the Enlightenment held no appeal for him; indeed, he was one of the first to employ the term 'romantic' in the modern sense of the term.[114] 'Romantic poetry,' he wrote, 'is a progressive universal poetry.'[115] Like Fichte, he sought to change the world by education, but for Schlegel, the teaching tool would be this romantic poetry:

> It [romantic poetry] is capable of the highest and broadest education; not only from the inside out, but from the outside in.[116]

Like Fichte's vision of philosophical education, Schlegel's romantic poetry knows no bounds; it 'always only becomes and can never be completed',[117] and, like Fichte's *Ich*, romantic poetry is free, for 'the will of the poet suffers no law over itself'.[118]

But, what kind of poetry is best for this education of the human race? Modern poetry, like modern man, presented Schlegel with a picture of internal discord. The various disciplines have forgotten their aims; poetry has forgotten that beauty is its final goal, and

> Philosophy is poeticized and poetry philosophized; history is treated as verse, while the latter is as history.[119]

There results an intellectual anarchy, reflecting an era made incomplete by the divisions within itself. The main challenge is to restore unity to the mind of the human race. How would this be done? Through the study of ancient, especially Greek, poetry.

Like Schiller, Schlegel envisaged ancient Greece as a golden age when man existed in perfection. Man was whole; all his faculties were developed in a full, interdependent manner. Study of the writers from this age could restore harmony to modern man, releasing him from the 'divisions and isolation of the human powers' which Schlegel saw as the 'real original sin of modern education'.[120] According to Schlegel, education also suffered from the dominance of the Enlightenment with its superficial view of the human mind. Instead of genuine development of the human soul, education in the Enlightenment offered only finishing in the social graces, lacking in 'unity and scholarship'.[121] In contrast, Schlegel argued that 'the study of Greeks and Romans is a school of the great, noble, good and the beautiful of humanity'.[122] Armed with this kind of education, man can achieve his great, noble calling. Education is an end in itself. All thought of utility in education means nothing:

> One lives not to be happy, or to do his duty, but to educate himself.[123]

The pre-professional ideal has no place; neither does Kant's emphasis on duty. Instead, Schlegel, a true founder of Romanticism, tied education directly to his grandiose image of man. 'Each good person,' writes Schlegel, 'becomes more and more God. To become God, to be human, to educate the self, are expressions which mean the same thing.'[124]

Education, then, is the act of self-creation. It is the progressive, and perhaps unending, drive of the self to achieve full power and unity. And, to Schlegel, there is no better way to go about this education than to study the ancient Greeks, who represented man at his most unified and divine. The interest in antiquity which Heyne fostered at Göttingen found a home at Jena. This, together with Goethe's ideal of *Bildung* and idealist philosophy, gave a new impetus to university studies and helped give rise to a new Idea, a new set of goals, for the university.

Classical studies, long a part of German university curricula, would indeed take on a new importance in the nineteenth century. The numerous critical editions of ancient and medieval texts which nineteenth-century German scholarship produced stand as testimony to a fine tradition of philology. In many cases these editions have remained standards for more than a century. It remains an open question, though, whether much of this scholarship was done in the tradition of Schiller and Schlegel: that of presenting a challenge to modern man via facing him with the greatness of the past. The *Wissenschaft* of classical scholars had become very entrenched by the end of the century, with well-paid professors employing armies of *Privatdozenten* to produce an edition or a new concordance for a classical author. Nietzsche, with his *The Birth of Tragedy*, attempted to provide a new aesthetic for drama drawn in part from his classical studies. But as a result of this work, the academic community rejected him, causing students to avoid his courses at Basel. Fritz Ringer's argument that the fresh ideas of the dawn of the century became ossified by its close seems quite telling here. Teaching, moreover, took second place to research, and one doubts if Fichte or his followers would have approved.

But what of other *Wissenschaften*? Did they have a place in the romantic Idea of the university? At least one author of the Jena school believed that they did. This man, in 1802, presented the most complete statement of the romantic Idea of the university to come out of this period. It was also a valedictory statement; Fichte, the Schlegels and Novalis had already gone when he delivered it, and, only three years later, Napoleon would crush the Prussians on the outskirts of town. The author of this work was the youngest member of the Jena School, Friedrich Schelling.

Born in 1775, Schelling was eight years younger than A. W. Schlegel, five years younger than Hölderlin, and three years younger than Friedrich Schlegel and Novalis.[125] Even as a boy, he was always the youngest in his circle. His gifts enabled him quickly to outstrip the schools in his area, so his father, a noted theologian and master of oriental languages, took the boy's education upon himself. When only 15 he enrolled at the University of Tübingen, where he entered into close friendship with Hegel and Hölderlin, both students there.

Schelling's academic life featured numerous changes of interest, resulting in a breadth of knowledge perhaps unsurpassed in his day. The young Schelling originally went to Tübingen to study theology and biblical exegesis. His natural gift for the study of languages, combined with his earlier training in Greek and Hebrew which his father gave him, made him a prime candidate for Biblical studies; besides, it was what his father wanted him to do. But contact with new people and ideas changed his interests. The new epistemology of Kant was in the air; so, too, were the new ideas about history and culture of Herder and Lessing. But most of all, the revolution in France (Schelling came to Tübingen in the autumn of 1790) convinced the brilliant youth that a new age had dawned.

He thus turned from Biblical exegesis to a critical examination of myth and culture. In the autumn of 1792, he wrote a paper arguing that the Bible was not just divine revelation, but a mythical covering for secret Egyptian knowledge.[126] Influenced by Herder, Schelling believed that myths, instead of being mere superstitions, were actually expressions of the mentality of past ages and peoples. The Enlightenment dismissed myths as enemies of reason; Schelling and the Romantics embraced them as expressions of the spirit of the past. But this work with myths was in reality tied to Schelling's earlier work in Biblical exegesis, for it was the study of Biblical and ancient texts (in the original languages) which excited his interest.

Schelling's field of study changed again during his last years at Tübingen. Hegel and Hölderlin left Tübingen in the autumn of 1793. During the following year, Schelling did not remain immune to the new teachings of Fichte. As early as September 1794, Schelling wrote a vehement defence of Fichte's philosophy, 'Über die Möglichkeit einer Form der Philosophie überhaupt' (On the Possibility of a Form of Philosophy in General). During the following year, he published 'Vom Ich als Prinzip der Philosophie' (On the Self as a Principle of Philosophy). Even the title of this work was Fichtean; so were its contents. Schelling portrayed the *Ich*, the Self, as the true foundation of all things. All things which humans sense are mere accidents, mere reflections, of the real substance of the *Ich*.[127] Philosophy, and especially speculative metaphysics, had by now displaced his earlier interest in philology.

But Schelling's interests would broaden still further. He took his theology examination at Tübingen in the summer of 1795. But theology as such no longer interested him; it was too narrow, too confining, too defined by tradition. The young man, moreover, believed a new age of humanity was opening, one in which intellectual freedom and progress would play important roles. Visits to Schiller and the Schlegels at Jena (1795) confirmed his attachment to Fichte's ideas. But the newest field, the one that offered the greatest possibilities for progress, was natural science.

Schelling wished to take the philosophical structure of Fichte's ideas and apply them to the natural world. He accepted Fichte's notion that the *Ich* was the determinant of nature. He wrote in 1795:

A secret, wonderful ability helps us to draw ourselves back from temporal flux into time to our innermost selves . . . and there, under the condition of changelessness, to look at the eternal in us. . . . We are not lost in the point of view of the objective world, but it is lost in ours.[128]

But what was this 'hidden, secret ability', this *Ich*? Fichte envisaged it as reason, imagination and other faculties, all existing within the human mind and completely independent of the objects of experience. It was an expression not only of Reason within the individual, but of society as well. One may perhaps compare it to the collective subconscious of Jung's psychology, except that Fichte conceived of a collective *consciousness*, growing through its struggle to preserve itself against the 'Nicht-Ich' of the sensual world.

Schelling used the term 'Ich', but as his interest in science grew, he changed the meaning of the term. In 1798, Schelling published 'Von der Weltseele, eine Hypothese der höheren Physik zu Erklärung des allgemeinen Organismus' (On the World Soul, a Hypothesis of Higher Physics in Explanation of the Universal Organism). This work presented the concept of the *Weltseele*, the 'World Soul', an organizing metaphysical structure to which all of nature belonged. The term 'Ich' now applied to this World Soul. The *Ich* thus no longer appeared in the consciousness of individuals or of civilization, but in the underlying structure of the natural world.

It was while developing the concept of the World Soul that Schelling came into direct contact with the Jena Romantics. He left Tübingen in the autumn of 1795; during the following year, he accepted work as a tutor in a noble family at Jena.[129] In 1798, he obtained a post at the University of Jena. Fichte needed some assistance; an interview with Goethe was arranged. Goethe was very impressed by the young man (who was only 23) and comforted by his belief that Schelling was no Jacobin.[130] Schelling had apparently left the political radicalism of his youth behind.

Schelling's arrival was another sign of Jena's special position in German academe. His father had tried in vain to get him a position at Tübingen. Schelling in fact expressed relief when this attempt fell through and was thankful to be spared 'too small an existence' at a university that he considered unworthy of his talents.[131] Schelling gladly accepted the post at Jena despite the fact that no stipend came with it. He wanted to be at the centre of German academics, and Jena was this centre.

When Fichte left Jena the following year, some saw the young Schelling as his rightful successor. But it was not to be. First of all,

Schelling, by contemporary accounts, lacked Fichte's great talents as a teacher. Fichte was headstrong but not without charm; Schelling appears to have been merely arrogant. Friedrich Schlegel referred to him as '*der Granit*', while his wife noted:

> He should really be a French general; he is not well fit for the lectern, even less so, I believe, for the literary world.[132]

At the lectern, his arrogance was apparent; so too, was his tendency to talk too fast and not really communicate to the students. Fichte was gone, there would be no fitting replacement. Schelling himself did not stay long, and left in 1803 with August Schlegel's former wife, Caroline.

But whatever his shortcomings as a teacher, Schelling left an important document in the development of the romantic Idea of the university: *On Academic Studies*. This book appeared in 1803 as a print edition of lectures given the previous year at Jena. This work sums up much of that which came before: the assault on vocationalism and careerism; the attempt to tie educational theory to Idealist philosophy, and the vision of a university as having a special role in society are all there. But unlike anything by Fichte or the Schlegels it also discusses at length the curriculum of the university.

Schelling shared many of the complaints aired by Kant and Fichte about the state of higher education. Early in the first lecture, he attacked a familiar target. 'Concern for universal culture,' he argued, 'is neglected in the individual's concern for his profession: the student trying to make himself a good lawyer or physician loses sight of the higher purpose of learning, which is to ennoble one's mind through science.'[133] The emphasis of professional education at the expense of study in the liberal arts remains a source of faculty displeasure. Like Schiller, Schelling was particularly disturbed by how the system wasted the talents of good students, pushing them into vocational tracks and giving them a contempt for *Wissenschaft*. Schelling also attacked an over-emphasis on memorization; empty pedantry; and, of course, carousing, rowdy students. But for all these complaints, Schelling offered essentially one solution: a more conscious realization of the inherent unity of all knowledge.

The depth of Schelling's belief in the World Soul, then, stands out clearly in the lectures on Academic Studies. He treated knowledge as an 'organic' whole; individual disciplines are only parts of the whole, branches of a single tree.[134] These branches only reflect, in the real world, the unified perfection of all knowledge which exists in the realm of the ideal. Beneath these particular branches lies 'unconditional' or 'archetypal' knowledge. And one must become aware of the existence of this pure, ideal knowledge before studying particular disciplines.

Schelling saw an analogy of this unity of knowledge in the structure of the human mind. Unlike many psychological theorist of this day, Schelling denied that the mind consists of tidy compartments known as 'faculties'. Most Romantics approved of faculty psychology, which experienced a resurgence in the early nineteenth century. Instead, Schelling argued that 'the essence of the soul is one. There are no faculties – they are assumed by a false psychological abstraction.'[135] A soul which exists in such unity must be developed by a curriculum stressing the unity of all knowledge.

The educational process for Schelling consists of a creative development of the whole soul by good teachers through the study of various disciplines. Some studies are particularly useful. Geometry, for example, 'clears the mind for purely rational cognition, independent of practical application'.[136] Philosophy also enjoys a special place in Schelling's curriculum. Schelling, though, manages to find room for many disciplines in his system. History, law and medicine have their place; moreover, Schelling's interest in the natural sciences appears as he discusses at length their roles in the curriculum. But Schelling takes pains to tie *every* discipline to the whole, the unity of knowledge. Faculty and students must keep the true goal of education always in mind:

> All rules which one can prescribe for students come together in one: Learn only in order to create yourself.[137]

The student must, through the study of his discipline, draw forth the image of his own soul, much as an artist does with raw clay.[138] Learning is an act of creation which arises out of a lively interest in the subject at hand and a recognition of that which ties it to everything else.

Schelling's special vision for the student brings with it an important role for the teacher as well. The teacher presents the whole of his discipline to the student. Teaching by rote is useless; instead, the teacher must 'build up the whole science, as it were, before the student's eyes'.[139] He must show the students how results are arrived at, and the process and method of his work. Consequently, the instructor must himself master his *Wissenschaft*. Although some, said Schelling, view universities merely as transmitters of knowledge, such cannot really be the case. A teacher worthy of the name cannot help others develop their souls through *Wissenschaft* if he has not done so himself. Only true scholars can be teachers. Only those who have gone through the creative process of mastering a *Wissenschaft* can guide others along the path.

Like Fichte, Schelling demanded that professors be granted freedom from interference. And, like Fichte, he envisaged the learned forming a class apart:

> The realm of the sciences is no democracy, much less an oligarchy, but an aristocracy in the noblest sense. The best should rule.[140]

An active professoriate dedicated to the various disciplines would cure the ills of the university. The lazy instructors will be weeded out by competition; rowdy students will leave and be replaced by zealous learners.[141] The ardent pursuit of the various *Wissenschaften* would thus improve teaching and create a better educational environment.

Schelling gave more importance to pure research than Fichte. Fichte's main works, including the *Wissenschaftslehre*, grew directly out of his teaching. But Schelling's grasp was broader, extending not only to philosophy, but to theology, classical philology, the natural sciences and medicine. His personal breadth of interests is reflected in *On Academic Studies*, for the last several chapters try to show the connection among all these disciplines and the unified whole of all knowledge. Fichte envisaged the learned primarily as great teachers; Schelling saw them as men who were great teachers *because* they were great *scholars*. Given his intense belief in the unity of everything – nature, the human soul and human knowledge – Schelling never seems to have entertained the possibility that research would dominate and leave teaching behind. As Fritz Ringer notes in *The Decline of the German Mandarins*, that is precisely what happened. Through the course of the nineteenth century, German professors went from being underpaid civil servants to demigods of research and the seminar.

Schelling and the other members of the Jena school envisaged nothing of the sort. They developed an Idea of the university based on a responsible and active professoriate heavily involved in teaching.

They promoted the arts and sciences of the lower, philosophical faculty, not as mere preparations for law theology or medicine, but as supremely worthy objects of study in and of themselves. But, except for Fichte, most Romantics had little taste for the rough-and-tumble politics of institutional change. Their reign at Jena was brief, and over several years before Napoleon's army appeared at the city gates. Fate smiled on them, though: they would get another chance to put this idea into practice – in Berlin.

# 3
# The Romantic Idea of a University in England

Nothing approaching the drama at Jena took place at Oxbridge in the early nineteenth century. Perhaps the main reason for this was that the English universities differed from those in Germany in both purpose and organization. Unlike the German universities, the two English ones were composed almost entirely of one faculty. As we have seen, the medical, legal and theological faculties existed only in vestigial form at Oxbridge. The *facultas artium* alone had a living role in the university. In England there could be no *Streit der Fakultäten*, no conflict of the faculties, for only one faculty really existed. The equivalents of the upper faculties of German institutions had withered away. As a result, the arts faculty would not face the conflicts which helped its German counterparts develop a sense of importance and strength. After all, it was the conflict between faculties which egged on Wolf, Kant and Fichte.

This is not to say that all was quiet in the English universities. They faced strong criticism from the outside, beginning with a series of articles published in the Whig journal, *The Edinburgh Review*, in 1809–10. Critics abounded within university walls as well. Although some changes were made between 1800 and 1850, these were gradual and piecemeal. There was nothing comparable to the rise of the philosophical faculty at Jena in the 1790s (which, as will be discussed, carried over into other German institutions). Instead, the English arts faculties remained tied to the Anglican tradition and to the collegiate system. So, too, did many of the English Romantics.

Another reason that the Romantics had a more conservative influence in English universities was that they tended to form groups outside the university environment. As in the eighteenth century, London remained the cultural centre. Coleridge and Wordsworth, meanwhile, found inspiration in nature, while Byron and Shelley travelled abroad. None of the major English Romantics made an English university his permanent home; while they attended the universities, they tended not to remain and teach after earning a degree. They had no desire to be celibate fellows in colleges, so they sought homes instead amidst the excitement of London or the quiet peace of the North Country.

Most of the English Romantics did none the less obtain an education at Oxbridge. Keats was the main exception since he pursued medical studies in London. But Byron, Shelley, Southey, De Quincey, Wordsworth and Coleridge all spent at least some time at these universities. Though most expressed dissatisfaction with the universities while they attended them, they did not, as a whole, advocate any real changes in the structure of Oxbridge. The social and political conservatism of many English Romantics (especially Wordsworth, De Quincey and Coleridge) carried over into their Idea of a university.

Of all the English Romantics, Byron perhaps enjoyed Oxbridge the most. The reason was simple: Byron was a libertine and (at least before the advent of evangelicalism) Oxbridge was a libertine's paradise. Byron came up to Trinity College, Cambridge, in 1805, complaining all the while that his guardians had failed to send him to his first choice, Oxford.[1]

But Byron was hardly suffering. He boasted of having one of the best allowances of any student.[2] The wealthy young nobleman seems to have lived quite well; soon after he arrived, he ordered his private cellar sent:

> Dear Sir – I will be obliged to you to order me down 4 Dozen of Wine, Port, Sherry, Claret, and Maderia, one Dozen of each . . .[3]

Lord Byron was already living the life of sensual pleasure which became his trademark. 'My life here,' he wrote in 1807, 'has been one continued routine of Dissipation . . .'[4] He was reputed to have a resident female companion whom he dressed in men's clothing and passed as his brother.[5] Whether this tale is true or not, it fits with his character. It also fits with the character of Cambridge of that day that Byron was never taken to task by university or collegiate authorities. A rake presented no threat to the status quo and was left unmolested.

One wonders, then, if Lord Byron did any studying at Cambridge.

He did stay on to take an M.A. in July 1808, and towards the end of his college career he wrote to a friend and gave a description of his academic achievements:

> Of the Classics I know about as much as most Schoolboys. . . . Of law enough to keep within the Statute . . . of Mathematics enough to give me the headache without clearing the part affected, of Philosophy, Astronomy, and Metaphysicks, more than I can comprehend, and of Common Sense, so little, that I mean to leave a Byronic prize at each of our Alma Matres for the first Discovery . . .[6]

The irony was that although Lord Byron freely admitted that he drank and fooled his way through Cambridge, he could not help but pass judgement on the universities for encouraging vice. He called them 'wretched' places, with 'a villainous Chaos of Dice and Drunkeness'.[7] His biggest complaint was of stagnation:

> The Muses, poor Devils, are totally neglected, except by a few musty old *Sophs* and *Fellows*, who however agreeable they may be to *Minerva*, are perfect antidotes to the *Graces*.[8]

Nowhere did Lord Byron vent his frustration more than in his poem, 'Thoughts Suggested by a College Examination' (1807). Lord Byron's principal complaint in this poem was that Cambridge had sacrificed the present to the past and had choked the life out of learning in the process. Dons, says Lord Byron, inspire fear but no wonder in students. They produce a student

> Who, scarcely skill'd an English line to pen,
> Scans Attic metres with a critic's ken.
>
> ll. 11–12

Such a youth, argued Byron, could feel nothing stirring, heroic or active in literature or history. He would remain ignorant of the glories of England's past, both as lived by her greatest kings and as described by 'Avon's bard' (l. 22). Worst of all are the fellows, who

> Linger in ease in Grant's sluggish shade;
> Where on Cam's sedgy banks supine they lie
>
> ll. 48–9

and who are dull, arrogant, rude and bigoted defenders of the Church.

Byron thus reiterated many of the complaints levied at the university by Gibbon, Knox and others of the eighteenth century. He had few new criticisms to offer and no constructive suggestions to make. Universities simply did not matter to him. Like many before him, he came, had a good time, complained about the lax morals (while joining in the fun himself), took a degree and left. For all his personal wildness, Byron was quite traditional in his treatment of the universities. He saw them for what they were, but did not demand anything new from them. He wanted a place where he could socialize, write and engage in some youthful dissipation; Cambridge of his day was just such a place.

Other Romantics had a greater sense of disgust at the condition of Oxbridge. As the son of a Unitarian minister, William Hazlitt did not have access to the English universities. He none the less found time to condemn them, arguing that 'our universities are, in a great measure, become cisterns to hold, not conduits to dispense, knowledge'.[9] Robert Southey baulked at subscription to the Thirty-nine Articles at Oxford; he later said that all he learned to do there was row and swim.[10] Southey never took a degree; instead, he met Coleridge in 1794 and left that year to join in Coleridge's scheme to establish a utopian colony in America. The scheme (called 'pantisocracy') never came off and Southey did not return to Oxford.

Another Romantic who cut his academic career short was Shelley. Like Byron, Shelley came from genteel stock. His grandfather was a baronet and his father was an MP for Sussex. After attending Eton, Shelley came to his father's alma mater, University College, Oxford, in 1810. Shelley's father had some hopes for his son but was soon bitterly disappointed; their lengthy strife began while Shelley was at Oxford.

Little in the university curriculum interested Shelley. He had limited patience with mathematics, and his youthful interest in science (especially in Galvinism) found no outlet in established courses. Shelley's political radicalism (acquired largely through a study of Godwin's works) was at odds with the aristocratic, socially stratified atmosphere of Oxford. But this same radicalism did spur a zealous pursuit of logic. Shelley loved to argue and believed he had found an environment where unrestrained debate was permitted. Shelley would learn to his detriment that Oxford in fact did not provide such an environment.

Shelley's growing radicalism found its chief expression in religion. He became a virulent detractor of Christianity, writing at one point:

Oh! how I wish I were the Antichrist! That it were mine to crush the demon [of Christianity]; to hurl him into his native hell, never to rise again.[11]

Shelley's father demanded that he refrain from such expressions and hired a clergyman to guide the youth away from atheism. But Shelley's insistent urge to argue got the better of him. He had tired of the placid assurances then offered as proofs of God's existence – particularly (one supposes) of the design argument employed by Paley and the university authorities. Shelley's desire to promote debate on the existence of God proved his undoing at Oxford.

Driven by these religious doubts, Shelley published *The Necessity of Atheism* in February 1811. In some ways the title was more provocative than the contents. Shelley did not argue that God's existence had been disproved; instead, he maintained that the existing proofs of His existence were inadequate and that from a logical standpoint one must refuse to believe in God until better proofs were advanced. Shelley himself sent copies of *The Necessity of Atheism* to several important church officials in order to elicit a response from them. He envisaged his spicy little pamphlet shaking Oxford from its intellectual doldrums by generating a debate on a vital topic.

But trouble came in the person of Edward Copleston, Master of Oriel College. Copleston had just finished defending Oxford against an assault from that outspoken proponent of Scottish Whiggery, *The Edinburgh Review*. He was in no mood to allow an Oxford man to bring discredit to the institution with such a pamphlet. Shelley foolishly sent him a copy, which Copleston took straight to the Master of University College. Although he had published the pamphlet anonymously, Shelley made little effort to hide the identity of its author. The Master immediately summoned both Shelley and his best friend, Thomas Hogg. He asked both young men if they had written the pamphlet. When Shelley and Hogg refused to answer, they were expelled and given 24 hours to leave. The Master said that his grounds for the expulsions were 'contumacy in refusing to answer certain questions put to them' and 'repeated declining to disavow a publication entitled *The Necessity of Atheism*'.[12] Shelley and Hogg left, ending forever their association with the University.

This incident reveals much about Shelley's Oxford and about Shelley's dreams for it. As with Wesley, Shelley was guilty of being anti-social and too questioning of the religious status quo. Hogg's father complained about the failure of both young men to fit in with Oxford's social life:

> These two young men gave up associating with anybody else some months since, never dined at college, dressed differently from all others, and did everything in their power to show singularity . . .[13]

In Shelley's day, as in Wesley's, 'singularity' was something for which Oxford had no tolerance.

This singularity was intensified by Shelley's sense of mission. 'On account of the responsibility to which my residence at the university subjects me,' he wrote shortly before his expulsion, 'I hope that my every endeavour, insufficient as this may be, will be directed to the advancement of liberty.'[14] After he was expelled, Shelley wrote to his father to explain his actions. He argued that he had written the pamphlet to redress the weakness of the proofs for God's existence. He hoped for 'a satisfactory, or an unsatisfactory answer from men who had made Divinity the study of their lives . . .'[15] Shelley wanted 'an *answer* not expulsion'; he dreamed of argument, not punishment.[16] In all of this, Shelley seems more naive than anything else. He sincerely believed that the university not only *should have been*, but already *was*, a place of liberty that promoted free debate on any topic.

Shelley dreamed of a university that made room for singular characters such as himself. To him the university should have been a place where one could read what one wanted, live as one pleased and have the freedom to argue any topic whatsoever. It should have been a place where one could argue for atheism in the presence of a bishop. Though very young, Shelley could recognize the institutional sensitive spots of Oxford and set out to tread on them. But his Idea of a university as a place to follow the argument wherever it led was not yet prevalent in England. Kant and Fichte had formulated this concept in Germany, but such broad academic freedom had not caught on in Shelley's country. Even many of his fellow Romantics had no time for such a notion. This was particularly the case with the Lake Poets.

William Wordsworth, for one, had no desire to see a German-style *Wissenschaftsuniversität* in England. His attachment to nature was so strong that it eclipsed all other considerations. He always viewed his Cambridge days as an unimportant part of his life's story, overshadowed by time spent among lakes, heights and rugged shores.

But though he was not favourably impressed by Cambridge, he had no desire to tear it down and build it up again. His indifference to the university made this unnecessary; his social and political conservatism (which grew more pronounced with age) made it unthinkable.

Though not of gentle birth, Wordsworth came to Cambridge in 1787 (at the age of 17) with some distinct advantages. Orphaned at a very early age, he was cared for by various relatives until he went to Hawkshead, one of the best schools in the North. There he boarded with Ann Tyson, a kindly matron who gave Wordsworth the only maternal affection he ever really knew.

Hawkshead enjoyed a good relationship with Cambridge University and tended to send its pupils there rather than to Oxford. The school retained several exclusive scholarships at Cambridge colleges. In keeping with the Cambridge curriculum, Hawkshead put a special emphasis on mathematics and Newtonian physics (though the classics were by no means ignored).[17] The school thus offered Wordsworth the curriculum and the connections he would need for success at Cambridge.

Besides these advantages as a Hawkshead boy, Wordsworth enjoyed advantages peculiar to himself. His uncle, William Cookson, was a fellow at St. John's, the college Wordsworth chose to attend. Since Cookson planned to marry, the fellowship would probably become vacant just as Wordsworth was finishing his undergraduate studies. As a friend of William Pitt, Cookson probably had enough leverage to get Wordsworth the fellowship.[18] But there was only one catch: Wordsworth had to take an honours degree. Though he certainly had the talent to do so, Wordsworth chose not to. And this is where the careful plans for Wordsworth's future went awry.

Despite the advantages listed above, Wordsworth faced some serious disadvantages at Cambridge. First among these was social discrimination. No matter how promising his intellect, Wordsworth remained the North Country orphan boy. He almost certainly had a noticeable regional accent which would win him no social favour. He was moreover, a sizar, the equivalent of the modern work study student. As such, he received the worst quarters (right above the kitchen where he could hear the cooks fighting), ate from the leavings of the fellows' table and endured all the snobbishness that Georgian Cambridge had to offer.[19] Cambridge, like Oxford, valued social distinctions highly, and Wordsworth simply did not have the right rank to fit comfortably into the Cambridge scene.

But there had been many sizars before Wordsworth – and many North Country men. Paley came from Yorkshire, and the professors of chemistry and common law of Wordsworth's day also hailed from the North. More was amiss than Wordsworth's social standing.

The problem also did not lay in Wordsworth's abilities. There is every indication that he read a good deal while at Cambridge and paid particular attention to ancient and modern languages.[20] He did abhor mathematics; and this alone could have kept him from an honours degree. Wordsworth, however, never took the honours examination in mathematics. He did not try for an honours degree and fail; instead, he decided early on not even to compete for an honours degree at all. A look at the reasons behind this decision reveals much about what he thought universities should be.

Judging from his recollections in *The Prelude* (1805), Wordsworth never felt at home in Cambridge. He actually said little about what he studied there. Of student life and all its 'small jealousies and triumphs good or bad' he chose to make 'short mention', for

> Things they were which then
> I did not love, nor do I love them now:
> Such glory was but little sought by me
> And little won.

> IV. 68–72

As Ben Ross Schneider argues, Wordsworth felt called to something outside of college walls. He always saw himself as a mere visitor at the university and felt

> a strangeness in my mind;
> A feeling that I was not for that hour,
> Nor for that place.

> III. 79–81

He often went walking on his own, but still felt separated from the 'shapes sublime' of his youth (III. 102). He was the *homo viator*, a 'chosen son' of nature, and was out of place in the artificial environment of the university. Like Milton (whom he deeply admired), Wordsworth at university was an eagle in a cage.[21]

But given the university calendar, Wordsworth gained his freedom from this cage when he left for the summer. He immediately returned to Hawkshead, where Ann Tyson welcomed him back with open arms. So, too, did the beauty of the North Country. Here, Wordsworth could come once again into his own:

> Gently did my soul
> Put off her veil, and, self-transmuted, stand
> Naked as in the presence of her God.[22]

The soul needed no colleges, tutors or universities to grow and change. It was 'self-transmuting', and found its own way so long as it was in a procreative natural environment. In the North, Wordsworth found

> How life pervades the undecaying mind,
> How the immortal soul with godlike powers
> Informs, creates, and thaws the deepest sleep
> That time can lay upon her...

> IV. 155–8

The soul was self-directing, self-awakening and (it would seem) self-educating. The 'deepest sleep' was the sleep brought upon the soul by a year at Cambridge, where Wordsworth wasted months in 'submissive idleness' (III. 669). Nature helped the soul to awaken from this slumber and grow to know its powers.

But how did nature help the soul to grow? Through the 'shapes sublime' which she presented to the senses. The concept of the sublime, of natural forces overwhelming the senses, was hardly a new one. It went back to at least the first century AD, when a Greek critic (once reputed to be named Longinus) published a work entitled *De Sublimate*. Long neglected, this little treatise was redis-covered in the Renaissance and became very popular in the eighteenth century.

According to *De Sublimate*, the sublime process occurs when a work of art causes the mind to grasp grand and powerful objects and conceptions. This process uplifts the soul, for

> it is a fact of Nature that the soul is raised by true sublimity, it gains a proud step upwards, it is filled with joy and exultation, as though itself had produced what it hears.[23]

Through the sublime, great artists demonstrate that nature considers man 'no low or ignoble animal', but a wonderful being who can observe all there is of her.[24] Indeed, the capacity for the sublime is the most ennobling attribute men have, for 'other qualities prove those who possess them to be men, sublimity raises them almost to the intellectual greatness of God'.[25]

By the latter half of the eighteenth century, seeking the sublime experience had become quite fashionable. Hundreds flocked to Mont Blanc and other places of grand natural beauty, hoping to experience at first hand the illumination of the sublime.

Numerous treatises appeared which discussed the sublime; as always, some had more lasting value than others. Immanuel Kant dealt with the subject twice. Early in his career, he completed his *Observations on the Feeling of the Beautiful and the Sublime*, a brief work which is far more accessible and readable than most of his writings. Much later, he dealt with it in a more typically Kantian fashion in his *Critique of Judgment*. Edmund Burke, meanwhile, wrote his own treatise on this topic in the 1750s. Both discussed how natural forces could overwhelm the senses and fill human hearts with a sense of the 'awful'. Burke presented the sublime as a destructive force, for it created 'that state of the soul, in which all its motions are suspended'.[26] Kant, on the other hand, emphasized how the human mind could use this sense of awe to its advantage and derive new strength in overcoming it.

In many ways, Wordsworth's vision of the sublime process reminds one of Longinus' and Kant's. Though he honoured the forces of nature, man was at the centre. To Wordsworth, the sublime experience did not arrest the faculties or annihilate them, but brought them to their fullest potential. It was the key to Wordsworth's thoughts about education, and underlay his response to the university environment.

Wordsworth developed his ideas not in a philosophical treatise, but in his magnificent poem, *The Prelude*. He made numerous revisions of it through much of his life, but wrote the bulk of it in 1804–5 with his friend Coleridge in mind. It did not appear in print until shortly before his death in 1850. Over the years, critics have referred to it as an 'epic'; but it is not about the founding of a nation, or (as in the case of *Paradise Lost*) the genesis of the human race, but the development of a soul and of the ideas which fed it.

In the course of this private epic, Wordsworth presents a remarkably clear image of the sublime. In the sixth book, he describes how he decided to go on a grand tour of Europe after a lacklustre term at

Cambridge. He had heard of all the sublime places, and actively sought the sublime experience, as had many others. In the course of his journey, he came to the ultimate Mecca of sublimity-seekers: Mont Blanc. When he first gazed upon it, he immediately felt that something was wrong: instead of overpowering him, the mountain presented an all-too-real 'soulless' image, which supplanted the richer one drawn beforehand in his mind's eye.[27] He nevertheless trudged onward through the great alpine passes, for he wanted desperately to believe in the sensual sublime of the eighteenth century, in the sublime which rested in nature and not man, which spoke through the senses, not the imagination. The wavering pilgrim then discovers that he has crossed the Alps, realizing, to his dismay, that going to the right place does not guarantee a rapturous encounter with nature.[28]

But through this disappointment came, in the ensuing decade, a great discovery:

> Imagination! – lifting up itself
> Before the eye and progress of my song
> Like an unfathered vapour, here that power,
> In all the might of its endowments, came
> Athwart me . . .

VI. 525–9

The sublime was thus 'unfathered' – it came about not from an overpowering of the faculties, but through their development.

Through his discussion of the sublime, Wordsworth gave man a glory even exceeding that of nature. He seemed to harken back to Longinus' position, for the sublime elevated man instead of annihilating him *à la* Burke. This anthropocentric vision appears clearly at the end of *The Prelude*; for while Milton (whom Wordsworth deeply admired) wished, in his epic,

> to assert Providence
> And justify the ways of God to men . . .

Wordsworth wanted to instruct his readers on

> how the mind of man becomes
> A thousand times more beautiful than the earth
> On which it dwells

XIII. 446–8

The human mind lives in this 'beauty exalted' because 'it is itself/ Of substance and fabric divine'.[29] The sublime thus becomes a tool to help man grow greater than nature by evoking the most divine of his many faculties: imagination.

These thoughts on the sublime came to Wordsworth long after he left Cambridge. They were not the reactions of youth, but the conscious thoughts of a mature man. By 1805, Wordsworth (in his mid-thirties) could say, 'I knew the worth of what I possessed' (IV. 351). But what he possessed after Cambridge was rich: a great creative imagination and a beautiful natural environment, which nurtured it and gave it freedom.

It is little wonder, then, that Wordsworth responded poorly to the established curriculum of Cambridge. He had by his own admission been 'spoiled' by nature, and was 'ill-tutored for captivity' (III. 359–63). And after his first year, his return to Hawkshead had resolved in his mind his sense of mission as a poet. With such a mission, wasting time in pursuit of mere worldly honours would, to Wordsworth, have been a sin. So he studied no mathematics, but instead read poetry and poets in ancient and modern languages to prepare himself better for his role in life – not as fellow or clergyman, but as the greatest poet in English of his age.[30] But the laxity of Cambridge's system served his ends. Freed from the need to study for honours, Wordsworth could study as he wished, knowing that only a feeble examination stood between him and a poll degree.

One would think that Wordsworth was wholly indifferent to the Idea of a university. The university was the means to social advancement rather than to an education in the ways of the soul, which Wordsworth craved. After he gave up the pursuit of an honours degree, his relatives and guardians despaired of his future. Even his sister Dorothy (who later joined in his life of poetic creativity) expressed concern in 1790:

> I am very anxious about him just now, as he will shortly have to provide for himself. Next year he takes his degree; when he will go into orders I do not know, nor how he will employ himself . . .[31]

Wordsworth did take a poll degree, which, of course, would never be good enough for a fellowship. Academic honours went instead to his younger brother Christopher, who eventually became Master of Trinity College. Christopher was reputed to have all the hallmarks of the successful university man and it seems indeed that he fitted the mould nicely. Diligent, loyal, dull and uncreative, he found a permanent home in the social and intellectual structures of Cambridge.

But the remarkable thing about William Wordsworth was the way in which he could find accommodation with the very traditions he seemed to be rejecting. In *The Mirror and the Lamp*, M. H. Abrams takes pains to point out how much Wordsworth's poetry owed to eighteenth-century ideas. Similarly, when discussing Wordsworth's time at Cambridge, Schneider remarks:

> The common hypothesis that Wordsworth owed much to the tradition that he appeared to be rejecting is not weakened here, but verified.[32]

Despite his disaffection with Cambridge, Wordsworth never advocated radical changes in its curriculum or structure. He did have an idealized version of what it should be, but this did not imply a complete rejection of what it was.

In the midst of describing his Cambridge years in *The Prelude*, Wordsworth briefly presented his Idea of a university:

> ... I
> Methinks could shape the image of a place
> which with its aspect should have bent me down
> To instantaneous service, should at once
> Have made me pay to science and arts
> And written lore, acknowledged my liege lord,
> A homage frankly offered up like that
> Which I had paid to Nature.
>
> III. 380–7

How could this place have transferred Wordsworth's allegiance to nature? By striking at the soul as nature did, with the sublime. Such a place would need to touch the heart inside and out, for

> Youth should be awed, possessed, as with a sense
> Religious, of what holy joy there is
> In knowledge if it be sincerely sought
> For its own sake
>
> II. 396–9

Possessed by this sublime experience of a thirst for knowledge, students would lead lives of Spartan simplicity, put away their 'trappings' and be stripped

> abashed
> Before antiquity and stedfast truth
>
> III. 402–3

One is reminded of Fichte proclaiming the glory of the scholar's vocation by comparing it to the mighty forces of nature.

Wordsworth also shared Fichte's distaste for the laziness and loose living associated with student life of the eighteenth century. As a former sizar, Wordsworth expressed dissatisfaction with the emphasis on appearance and class stratification then so prevalent at Oxbridge (more so than at German institutions). But nowhere did he advocate radical changes in the curriculum or the political structure of universities. Nor did he wish to change their fundamental role as seminaries of the Anglican Church. Indeed, one of Wordsworth's major concerns was that the emphasis which 'Presidents and Deans' placed on 'officious doings' (such as enforced chapel attendance) would

> bring disgrace
> On the plain steeples of our English Church
> Whose worship, 'mid remotest village trees
> Suffers for this.
>
> III. 420; 424–6

Ridding Cambridge of vanity and hypocrisy would return it to a pristine simplicity, in which young men could develop their intellectual and moral faculties. The university could become 'a sanctuary for our country's youth' (III. 440) and offer a pure education not unlike that which nature gave to Wordsworth himself. By filling the young with sublime awe, it could preserve the religious and moral fibre of the nation. Thus was a dream of the university presented, a conservative dream, looking not towards a utilitarian ideal, but to a moral and (ultimately) Christian one. Wordsworth was not alone; in later years, other Lake District writers expressed similar sentiments, but in more direct and explicit ways. One such was Thomas De Quincey.

Although born to a wealthy family, De Quincey faced a good deal of hardship during his lifetime. He was, in a word, dissipated. His irregular personal life (including a severe addiction to opium) was notorious. He is chiefly remembered not for his poetry, but for his memoirs of his own drug-distorted life. Yet despite his dissolute habits, he was a staunch defender of the Church of England and of his alma mater, Oxford.

While still a youth, De Quincey ran away to London and found his only solace there with the whores of Oxford Street. Like Shelley, he survived by borrowing against of his expectations and keeping one step ahead of creditors. De Quincey was eventually reconciled with his family and went to Worcester College, Oxford, in 1803.

De Quincey seems to have fitted into the Oxbridge system little better than did Shelley. According to a memoir published in 1835, he had originally wished to go to Christ Church, but went to Worcester instead merely because the 'caution money' (a kind of security deposit) was less there.[33] As for his tutor, De Quincey claims that they met only once – by chance in the quadrangle. During this meeting, the tutor asked the young scholar what he had been reading. Though De Quincey had in fact been studying the metaphysical works of Parmenides, he felt it best to give the tutor a convenient lie and said that he had been reading Paley. 'AH! an excellent author' was the tutor's response.[34] According to De Quincey, the two never exchanged another word.

Given this lack of tutorial guidance, De Quincey (like Byron and Wordsworth) spent his days studying what he wished and ignoring the established curriculum. He read a good deal of English literature and German philosophy. He of course shared this interest in German idealist thought with Samuel Coleridge, and the two men became friends after they first met in 1807. De Quincey also had the misfortune to share Coleridge's taste for opium, which undoubtedly contributed to his erratic behavior.

Nowhere was this instability better exemplified than when he stood for his degree. De Quincey decided to go for an A. B. with honours and actually went so far as to complete the written component of his examination. But he left the examination in terror when faced with *viva voce* proceedings. Insecure, uninterested in mathematics and (almost certainly) already addicted to opium, he simply could not face his examiners.[35]

But De Quincey had none the less gained something important at Oxford: a deep appreciation for the poetry of Wordsworth. His admiration was so deep that he moved north, to Grasmere, to be nearer to Wordsworth and Coleridge, and even occupied Dove Cottage after the Wordsworths vacated it. Soon, De Quincey joined William and Dorothy Wordsworth on their perambulations around the Lake District. De Quincey's personal habits, however, eventually proved too much for the Wordsworths. His drug habit worsened, and he sired a child with a local woman, whom he later married. As time passed, De Quincey (like Coleridge) became estranged from Wordsworth. De Quincey's personal life, however, proved to be a literary windfall; his *Confessions of an English Opium Eater* (first published in 1822) gave him a permanent place in English letters.

After this work appeared, De Quincey took to writing as a means to earn money and published prose works on a multitude of topics. Among these was an article published in *Tait's Edinburgh Magazine* (1835) on the University of Oxford. Here De Quincey presented a refreshing viewpoint: while he acknowledged the problems of Oxford, he nevertheless defended his alma mater and offered a uniquely English romantic Idea of a university. This Idea corresponds strongly with that presented by Coleridge in his *On the Constitution of Church and State*.

De Quincey's article was inspired by talk of governmental intervention into university affairs. Oxford faced stiff published criticism throughout the first decades of the nineteenth century, much of it in the pages of the *Edinburgh Review*. This first assault came in 1810 and was parried by Bishop Copleston. The second began in 1831 and continued until 1836; this time, De Quincey was among Oxford's defenders. Since, as he noted, 'some roving commission may be annually looked for' (it actually did come in 1850), there needed to be an accurate, objective account of Oxford.[36]

De Quincey purported to be free of any vested interest in the university and thus to be capable of offering such an account:

> Oxford, ancient mother! hoary with ancestral honours, time-honoured, and haply, it may be, time-shattered power – I owe thee nothing.[37]

Yet while De Quincey might have had no direct ties to Oxford, he was a staunch defender of the cultural and political status quo of England. Unlike Shelley, he saw nothing wrong with Oxford as an Anglican seminary. Indeed, he saw little wrong with Oxford at all.

De Quincey defended even the most universally maligned aspects of Oxford life. It bothered him little that professors did not teach, for tutors did the real job of educating the young:

> if the existing Professors were *ex abundanti* to volunteer the most exemplary spirit of exertion . . . it would contribute but little to the promotion of academic purposes.[38]

De Quincey saw no particular advantage in the German style of professorships. German professors, he argued, put their students to sleep with their *wissenschaftlich* droning, but Oxford tutors offered their charges 'a real drill'. De Quincey also condemned the competitive nature of German academe, for he believed that such rivalry only made a 'whole kennel of scoundrel Professors ruin one another . . . all hating, fighting, calumnating each other, until the land is sick of its base knowledge mongers . . .'[39] A professor at a German university held his position 'not on his good behaviour, but on the capricious pleasure of the young men who resort to his market'.[40]

De Quincey's Idea of a university thus has little in common with either the German romantic Idea or with that enunciated by Adam Smith. De Quincey wanted no marketplace of ideas; that would sully and debase the sacred national institutions of learning. Nor was he particularly interested in *Wissenschaft* for its own sake, or in august, powerful, egotistical professors *à la* Fichte. Instead, he envisaged a university that stuck to its traditional role of bringing a proper moral education to the nation's youth.

De Quincey was even satisfied with the target most often singled out by Oxford's critics, the Oxford student. Yes, admitted De Quincey, they were high-born; yes, they often lived lives of luxury in an environment rife with class distinctions. But at least the English aristocracy (unlike that of Germany) expressed some interest in education instead of mere military training. It does indeed seem true that German universities attracted some commoners or even paupers (witness the lower-class origins of Kant, Fichte and Schiller) while Oxbridge remained the home of the noble and gentry classes. As a Tory, De Quincey saw nothing wrong with class distinctions in society or in the university. 'It is to the great honour, in my opinion, of our own country,' he argued, 'that those often resort to her fountains who have no motive but that of disinterested reverence for knowledge.'[41] He saw no need to open the door to petty bourgeois hoping to become civil servants or to dissenters from the established church. Instead, he saw universities as the place for sons of the landed classes to receive a traditional Anglican education.

Such a position also made De Quincey a defender of the colleges. Some (such as Sir William Hamilton in the *Edinburgh Review*) had argued that the dominance of the colleges over the university harmed education and the progress of knowledge by weakening the role of the professor. But De Quincey defended the collegiate system as best for the moral and spiritual education of the young. It was right for colleges to have fine libraries, quadrangles and halls; 'these vast piles . . .,' argued De Quincey, 'are applied to the personal settlement and domestication of the students.'[42]

The colleges, the tutors, the unchanging curriculum – all served to unite England with its past. They helped give her landed classes a sense of moral purpose and permanence. Such an organic, Burkean Idea of a university, here presented in broad outline by De Quincey, was developed much more fully by his friend and fellow opium eater, Samuel Taylor Coleridge.

One thing can safely be said about Samuel Coleridge: he was not a simple man. Though in his youth he often joined William and Dorothy Wordsworth on their walking tours of the Lake District, his constant suffering and convoluted speculations seem alien to their pastoral world. But perhaps Coleridge's very difficulties were what gave his thoughts on society and education their depth. The guilt and frustration which arose from his chronic illness, drug addiction and family problems drove him to ask questions about the responsibility of the self to God and society and to present an alternative to the dominant utilitarian ideal. In all of this, his thoughts on education loom large as a keystone to his critique of society and his prescription for its betterment.

The son of a Devonshire clergyman, Coleridge rebelled against the Church of England. Soon after he left Cambridge (without taking a degree) in 1794, Coleridge gave some political lectures which reflected sympathy for Jacobinism and a disdain for the Church. He bitterly attacked predestination for its capricious attitude towards the fate of individuals.[43] But he also attacked Anglicanism for its similarities to Catholicism, stating that 'he who sees any real difference between the Church of Rome and the Church of England possesses optics which I do not possess', for both 'SELL the Gospel and rob the poor'.[44] The idea that human souls needed redemption and salvation was an absurdity to the young Coleridge, as was the doctrine of the Trinity.[45] He had clearly absorbed the Unitarian beliefs which were then in vogue among some elements of England's youth.[46]

Age, and the bitter experience it sometimes brings, changed his views remarkably. In the same year that he gave the sermons referred to above (1795), Coleridge married Sara Fricker as part of a utopian scheme known as pantisocracy. The scheme failed; as did the marriage, for the Coleridges were permanently separated within a decade. The great hopes Coleridge had for the French Revolution were, moreover, dashed when he considered the bloodshed of the Terror and the despotism of Bonaparte. Far worse for Coleridge, his constant complaints of pain and poor health led to a dependence on opium. Despite repeated attempts to free himself from the grip of laudanum, Coleridge remained an addict from about 1803 until the end of his life.

Robert Barth, in *Coleridge and Christian Doctrine*, argues convincingly that these ill-tidings had a profound and lasting impact on Coleridge's life and outlook. His poetic powers left him – by 1800, *Cristabel*, *The Rime of the Ancient Mariner* and his other great poems lay behind him. More importantly, the loss of control over his life caused him to reconsider his earlier scorn for the idea of Christian redemption.

During his last two decades, then, Coleridge wrote pamphlets, essays, and 'Lay Sermons' designed to show how England needed the Christian (and, more specifically, Anglican) Church to function as a just society. In his *Biographia Literaria* (1817), Coleridge asserted that the aim of his entire literary output was to

> kindle young minds, and to guard them against the temptation of scorners, by showing that the scheme of Christianity, as taught by the liturgy and homilies of our Church, though not discoverable by human reason, is yet in accordance with it.[47]

Later in his life, Coleridge declared he was 'by preference a Member of the Church of England', because it was 'in its Articles, Liturgy, and intended Constitution and Organization the purest form of a Christian Church'.[48] Coleridge's way of looking at the self, society and, perhaps the most important link between the two, education, was greatly influenced by his growing attachment to the Anglican tradition.

Coleridge's discussion of the self reflects both his Anglicanism and his affinity for German idealist philosophy. His most explicit discussion of the ontology of the self appears in *Biographia Literaria*.

In tight, syllogistic argument, Coleridge proclaims the need for a self-grounding, singular truth upon which all other truth must rest. This truth, says Coleridge, is 'Sum, or I AM', which is 'spirit, self, self-consciousness'.[49] This statement compares well with Fichte's in the *Wissenschaftslehre* (1797):

> the self *posits itself*, and by virtue of this mere self-assertion it *exists*.[50]

Fichte, moreover, went through a sequence of logical statements similar to Coleridge's to arrive at this conclusion. But there remains a crucial difference between the two. Coleridge complains that Fichte's theory of the self

> degenerated into a crude *egoismus*, a boastful and hyperbolic hostility to Nature, as lifeless, godless, and altogether unholy.[51]

Something is needed beyond the merely human self-positing of Fichte: this is the self-positing of God, for

> in the very first revelation of his absolute being, Jehovah at the same time revealed the fundamental truth of all philosophy.

This revelation appears in Exodus 3:14: 'I AM that I Am.' This statement, in which the absolute I AM (God) declares its own existence, allows man, the 'conditional I', to do the same.[52] Through God, then, 'we live, and move, and have our being'.[53] Coleridge thus joins St. Paul, and makes all human self-consciousness, and all activity which springs from it, dependent on the will of God. He is intrigued by the ideas of Schelling, Fichte and Kant, but cannot accept their attempts to discuss human ontology without reference to revelation.

Coleridge presents an interesting way of looking at the individual, but holds strongly to the Aristotelian belief that man is nothing without society. Despite all the above discussion of self-consciousness, Coleridge maintained late in life that each individual 'seems to be influenced and determined and caused to be what he is, qualis sit – qualified, *bethinged* by a Universal Nature'.[54] Elsewhere, he is more specific:

> True philosophy is that the self is in and by itself a phantom ... because it is capable of receiving true entity by reflection from the Nation.[55]

The Nation – society, or, in his later usage, the State – plays a vital role in that it tells the individual who he is. Education serves the State by making its members into citizens. Political theory, embodying the purpose (the idea) of the State, has a hand in shaping educational theory.

Coleridge always had some criticism for contemporary society, but his complaints and his prescriptions for it changed with age. As a young man, he watched with awe and hope as the decrepit monarchy of France fell. After the Terror, his enthusiasm waned, but he still respected the ideals behind the violence: 'French Freedom is the Becon [*sic*] that while it guides us to Equality, should shew us the Dangers, that throng the Road.'[56] Fresh out of Cambridge, the young Unitarian shared in the hope that a new age had dawned, and that justice would come at last for the politically and economically oppressed. The change, he warned, must be complete, for a new spirit as well as new systems must arise. Even as a youth, Coleridge tried to communicate a theme prevalent in his later political thinking: reform of the heart, of individuals, must come before society as a whole can undergo needed moral reform.

As time passed, Coleridge left behind the upheaval in France and the Enlightened ideas associated with it, and became the theorist now considered a founding father of modern conservatism. Instead of a revolutionary overthrow of existing social structures, he sought a society which held unhealthy extremes in check by keeping in contact with its past. Religion would play an active role in this, and with it, the educational institutions of the Established Church.

This new emphasis on tradition appears strongly in Coleridge's works dating from 1816 onward. At about the same time he produced his *Biographia Literaria*, a diffusive review of his life and work, Coleridge wrote two 'Lay Sermons', which, as the title suggests, were religiously-oriented tracts aimed at the improvement of lay society. In the first of these, Coleridge turns harshly on his former compatriots, the Unitarians.[57] But he also sees a new and more dangerous enemy: the rise of 'a presumptuous and irreligious Philosophy' born of the middle class, which brings with it the 'conceit that states and governments might be and ought to be constructed as machines'.[58] This new product of the industrial era, the utilitarian ethic, robs the nation of its religious foundation and leads it to perdition. One of the Lay Sermons offers an alternative in its very title: 'The Statesmen's Manual, or, The Bible the Best Guide to Political Skill and Foresight'.

Why the Bible? In justifying this choice for a guide to political action, Coleridge presents an argument couched in the language of German idealism. Unlike any other guide, the Bible, says Coleridge, 'contains a Science of *Realities*' instead of abstractions.[59] It unites past and future, finite (man) with infinite (God). More importantly, it does not rest on the material conditions of any one age. Unlike those of utilitarianism, the Bible's teachings transcend the boundaries of any given era and present a vision of reality

> free from the Phenomena of Time and Space, and seen in the depth of *real* Being reveals itself to the pure Reason as the immanence of ALL in EACH.[60]

This statement, of course, abounds with Kantian language, complete with the distinction between the passing 'phenomenal' world and that of true Being, as well as the ties between 'ALL and EACH' which Kant emphasizes in his categorical imperative. But Coleridge takes these ideas and gives them his own religious bent. Instead of proposing a system of ethics based on reason alone, Coleridge argues that one already in existence, the Biblical one, is the only one which has absolute meaning beyond Time and Space. Much as he did with Fichte's theory of the Self, Coleridge here takes the language of German philosophy and gives it a Christian gloss.

Besides pointing to the Bible as a manual for the State, Coleridge offers some suggestions of his own for its improvement. No longer a devotee of French radicalism, by 1817, Coleridge, has nothing but praise for the English Constitution, and lauds 'the number and respectability of our sects; the pressure of our ranks on each other . . .'[61] But the new demon of the Commercial Spirit threatened to upset this balance.[62]

What could set society right? Force of arms? Coleridge never believed so; indeed, even as a youth, he said, 'if we would have no Nero without, we must place a caesar within us, and that caesar must be religion.'[63] The private man must be moral for a safe and just society to exist. This principle stands out in all Coleridge's work; even in 1795 he noted that 'general Illumination' must precede change[64] – a statement perhaps echoing Kant's sentiment in *What is Enlightenment?* (1784):

> the public can only slowly attain enlightenment. Perhaps a fall of personal despotism or of avaricious or tyrannical oppression may be accomplished by revolution, but never a true reform in ways of thinking.[65]

To Kant, Schiller and Coleridge, better individuals make for a better society. But how is this to come about? The various classes have their duty to this end: 'our manufacturers must consent to regulation', wrote Coleridge in 1817, 'our gentry must concern themselves with the *education* as well as the *instruction* of their natural clients and dependants.'[66] The answer is education, but clearly Coleridge had specific criteria about what *kind* of education, and this qualitative judgement reflects his beliefs about man as individual and man in society.

Put most simply, Coleridge, at least in his maturity, sought to restore the natural balance of society by creating an educated elite who could counter the rampant materialism of the industrial world. Like his German counterparts, Coleridge supported the development of fine minds in a university setting. The primary difference between Coleridge and, say, Schiller was the emphasis Coleridge placed on the religious aspects of that development. Schiller sought better people for a better society; Coleridge too wanted better people for a better society, but to serve the higher purpose of pleasing God by restoring the body politic to its divinely ordained form.

Coleridge valued mass education, but did not consider it an adequate means of reforming society. In his youth, he inveighed against elitism, arguing that 'the knowledge of the few cannot counteract the Ignorance of the Many', and urged reformers to 'go, preach the GOSPEL to the poor'.[67] But with time, he came to believe that such a general diffusion of simple knowledge was not enough. By 1816, he could observe Joseph Lancaster's system of mass literacy in action and argue that even if it succeeded – even if everyone in the realm could read and write – England would not have a national education.[68] Why? Because such a method cannot provide a nation with its leaders and is too caught up in the emptiness of secular empiricism to provide moral leadership. Society is losing its soul, not only due to a lack of regard for ancestry, but due to

> the general neglect of all the austerer studies; the long and ominous neglect of Philosphy; the usurpation of that venerable name by Physical and psychological Empiricism.

Even more telling is his final condemnation of the 'non-existence of a learned and philosophic Public, which is perhaps the only innoxious form of an imperium in imperio...'[69]

Clearly there were universities (Coleridge himself went to Cambridge), so why is such a class missing? Coleridge blames the dominance of Paley and others of his type at the university level. He is aghast at Paley's view that virtue is a form of self-love, born out of a realization that God can give pain or pleasure in the next life.[70] Much to Coleridge's dismay, this sensually-oriented view of God held sway 'at one of our universities, [presumably, Cambridge] justly the most celebrated for scientific ardor and manly thinking'.[71] To Coleridge, Paley's natural theology, his Christianized version of enlightened thought, only aids and abets the tyranny of materialism emerging from middle-class society.

In place of Paley must come the Bible, studied not in an un-thinking, fundamentalist fashion, but with constant reference to philosophic principles. Only this can provide a real education, which Coleridge, hearkening back to faculty psychology, says 'consists in *educing* the faculties and forming the habits'.[72] Only such develop-ment can endow the 'philosophic class' (which he later dubbed 'the clerisy') with faith, 'the realizing principle, the spiritual sub-stratum of the whole complex body of truth'.[73]

By 1817, then, Coleridge had formed the basic notions behind his vision of national education. He had drawn the battle-line be-tween his own Anglican Idealism and the then ascendant utilitarian approach. But Colerige's last work on the subject would wait until the early 1830s when he produced his final prescription for how to educate a nation in *On the Constitution of Church and State*.

This work, published in 1830, provides the most complete pre-sentation of Coleridge's vision for national education. It recapitulates and expands on his earlier discussions of how education meets the needs of man, his society and his Creator. The prescription it pro-vides for higher education became the model for those of the coming decades, such as the Cambridge Apostles, who were dissatisfied with the utilitarian ethos and tried to reform Cambridge and Oxford from within.

At the very beginning of this work, Coleridge attacks the utilitar-ian desire to fit man and society into objective laws. Laws, says Coleridge, are for the material world, the realm of mere things. But man can create, he is of a creative nature, and consequently is not subject to mere laws, but an 'Idea'.[74] But what is an Idea? Coleridge gives a definition with idealistic overtones indeed:

> That conception of a thing, which is not abstracted from any particular state, form, or mode, in which the thing may happen to exist at this or that time; nor yet generalized from any number

or succession of such forms or modes; but which is given by the knowledge of its ultimate aim.[75]

Man, his morality, his state and his Church therefore cannot be reduced to the mechanical formulae of law. Such institutions are growing, creative entities whose identity lay not in being, but becoming, not in their past, present or future state, but in the end for which they are intended. The outward shape of the Church and the State grow in an organic fashion, but their real substance, defined teleologically, remains constant and unchanged. Though Coleridge does not say so, the argument certainly seems to owe something to Burke.

Like Burke, moreover, Coleridge expressed an interest in maintaining the 'ancient' English constitution. He rejected Rousseau's concept of a 'Social Contract' formed to release man from an imaginary State of Nature, and believed instead that an 'ever-originating contract' in keeping with a nation's Ideas, will guide it properly.[76] The Idea of the State of England is one of balance. The interests of progress (which Coleridge identified with the capitalists) must be balanced with those of permanence – the landowning gentry and aristocracy.[77] While this thinking coincides with his earlier statements in the *Lay Sermons*, the emotionally charged language about the evils of unfettered materialism does not appear here. The theoretical and idealistic language of *On The Constitution of Church and State* leaves little room for such polemics.

Space nevertheless remains for a prescription to maintain this balance. To keep permanence and progression, past and present, in order, a National Church must preside over the cultivation of the minds of the state. This cultivation must rest

in the harmonious development of those qualities and faculties that characterized our humanity. We must be men in order to be citizens.[78]

A permanent class, the 'clerisy', must exist to cultivate individuals in this fashion. Coleridge deliberately chose a term with theological connotations, for in theology can be 'comprised all the main aids, instruments, and materials of NATIONAL EDUCATION, the *nisus formativus* of the body politic'. Filled with knowledge of theological truth, and hence of truth itself, the clerisy can set about its business: '*educing*, i.e., eliciting the latent *man* in all the natives of the soil . . .'[79]

With this, Coleridge gives a clear mission for universities. They are to develop and cultivate the country's leaders, who in turn can travel throughout the land and make people into adults and citizens. This will keep a nation in touch with its past; more importantly, it will build into its soul the moral values enunciated by the National Church.

Coleridge fills his writing in this work with the language of idealistic philosophy and faculty psychology. Universities clearly have an Idea of their own (creating and maintaining the clerisy) which in turn preserves the balance between permanence and progression needed if the State is to fulfil its Idea. Like Schiller, then, Coleridge speaks of cultivating individuals to serve the nation. Yet, one has the distinct impression that Coleridge remained satisfied with *raison d'être* of Oxford and Cambridge as they then existed: to serve as seminaries for the Anglican Church, producing the clerics needed for cures of souls throughout the country. The dissatisfaction he did express was with relatively new innovations, such as Paley and utilitarianism. Indeed, he showed no sign of wanting new universities at all, but instead wanted to restore the existing ones to their ancient purpose of theological and biblical education. Would these be *Bildungsuniversitaten*? Yes, but only if the Bible, the 'Statesman's Manual', is restored to its rightful place at the centre of the curriculum, along with the philosophical studies needed to aid in its interpretation.

Coleridge, then, uses some aspects of German thinking, but comes up with a model of the university that is much more conservative than that of his German counterparts. German Romantics believed in the need to start new universities from the ground up, much as they knew they would have to with a German constitution. Coleridge already had what he considered the finest nation-state and constitution on earth; its universities had only to be brought back to their original principles to achieve their purpose.

With its reaffirmation of existing institutions, Coleridge's model would heavily influence the next generation of university reformers in England. Its sense of moral vision appealed to an age of Evangelical revival, and to the Cambridge Apostles, the Oxford Movement and others who sought to reform the universities from within. It would offer a strong counter to the utilitarian pressure to make universities serve the secular needs of industrial society. But Coleridge's view was not unique among English Romantics; De Quincey and Wordsworth both shared in some aspects of it. This desire to preserve the colleges, tutors and other traditional aspects of Oxbridge life was in marked contrast to the wish of German Romantics to tear down and start anew. And nowhere was the drive of German Romantics to start again better exemplified than with the founding of the University of Berlin.

# 4
# The Romantic Idea of a University and the New Foundation in Berlin

Germans still look back with pride at the founding of the University of Berlin. Heinrich Steffens called it 'one of the most important movements in the history of modern Germany', and, even outside Germany, many see it as the birth of the modern university.[1] By the mid-ninteenth century, Berlin had become the flagship university in Germany and a model for new institutions worldwide. But how much did this institution partake of the romantic Idea of a university? It was, indeed, founded when Fichte, Schelling and other Romantics and idealist philosophers were at the height of their influence in German intellectual life. But it was also born in a time of bitter defeat for Prussia and an era filled with a level of confusion not seen in Germany since the Thirty Years' War. It was remarkable that the university came into being when it did; more notable still that it survived; and almost miraculous that it could achieve such fame in the decades after its founding. The romantic Idea of a university, born at Jena, was a midwife to this institution, but so were the immediate needs of the Prussian state.

Before the inception of the new university, the business of this state dominated the Prussian capital. Many outside Prussia saw Berlin as a cultural backwater, a city of soldiers. There was a royal academy of *Wissenschaften* there, but many considered this little more than an overgrown salon. Steffens remarked that 'The French superficiality introduced by Voltaire' had once dominated the capital, and that even when this spirit departed, the academy was 'half-German, half French' and brought 'little credit upon the city'.[2] Whatever the quality of the academy, it was not a teaching institution.

Great teachers had no place there, so Halle, Göttingen and (finally) Jena took first academic honours in Protestant Germany, leaving Berlin, the capital of the mightiest German state, a small role in German academic life.

All this began to change after 1800. Jena's glory was short-lived. After Fichte left in 1799, the romantic school there broke up. No real structural changes were made in the university. The full professors of the theological faculty retained control of the institution. Goethe, the Duke of Weimar's confidant for cultural affairs, gradually lost interest in university affairs. And as Jena's star set, Berlin's began to rise.

Among German intellectuals, Berlin gradually became the home for the homeless, a refuge for the discontented and the unemployed. Some from the University of Jena, including Fichte, Schelling and Wilhelm von Humboldt, found their way there. They discovered that they could eke out a living with public lectures or government support through the academy. As will be discussed below, many cringed at the very word 'university'; perhaps the very lack of a university in the Prussian capital attracted them. To those tired of the petty politics of university life, Berlin offered a place where one could be *frei aber einsam* (free, but alone). Helmut Schelsky suggests that this life of public lectures and informal discussions may have helped shape the university that eventually arose in Berlin. The atmosphere of freedom undoubtedly contributed to the drive to found an entirely new type of university there.[3]

These academic refugees, moreover, had an ally in one Prussian cabinet minister, Karl Friedrich Beyme. Beyme, the son of an army surgeon (an occupation also held by Schiller's father) studied at Halle and entered the Prussian bureaucracy when he was 23 years old. After Frederick Wilhelm III ascended the throne in 1797, Beyme replaced the reactionary Wöllner (Kant's old adversary) as the head of the King's Civil Cabinet.

Academics found a true friend in Beyme. He knew several languages and was a student of philosophy. He particularly admired Luther, Kant and Fichte; portraits of all three hung in his study.[4] One of his first acts was to improve the University of Halle. Already one of the leading German universities, Halle saw a resurgence under Beyme's guidance. He doubled the funds available for this university and worked to attract new talent there, including the noted theologian Schleiermacher.[5]

But Beyme's primary aim was to establish an entirely new type of educational institution in Berlin. He began by gradually coaxing new talent into the city. Fichte stayed in part because of Beyme's support. Beyme, moreover, worked to draw even greater names northward. He tried to bring Schiller, and might have done so but for Schiller's untimely death in 1805. Beyme even had dreams of drawing Goethe away from Weimar; though this, of course, never came to fruition.[6]

But what kind of institution would Beyme have created for such distinguished men? He produced a plan as early as 1802; though, no copy is now extant. It seems certain, though, that he accepted many of the concepts which came out of the Jena circle. He wrote in 1807 that he wished to create 'a general scientific teaching establishment free from all guild constraints'.[7] His use of 'guild constraints' (*Zunftzwang*) may seem a bit confusing. What he seems to be referring to is the entire old structure of the university – of student fraternities, dominant theological faculties, and the like. He accepted Schiller's notion that true scholars must be separated from materialistic students. Indeed, he never called his proposed institution a 'university' at all, for the term seemed too fixed in the past. He would, in fact, have placed existing universities on a level beneath that of the new Berlin institution, arguing that 'the existing universities must keep their separate organization for the so-called pre-professional studies'.[8] All of Beyme's ideas would be put to the severest test after Prussia's defeat by the Napoleonic army in 1806.

By coincidence, the town of Jena is famous not only for the events described in the second chapter, but also as the site of one of the bitterest defeats Prussia ever experienced. Prussia maintained a neutral stance at Austerlitz, but in 1806 chose to take on Napoleon's army alone. With antiquated tactics and slow supply trains, the Prussians were no match for Napoleon's forces. The armies met outside Jena on 14 October; by the evening, the Prussians had been routed with a loss of 45,000 killed, wounded or captured. Napoleon's army then moved northward and seized Berlin.

The following year, Napoleon and Tsar Alexander signed the famous treaty of Tilsit. Prussia, now under French occupation, lost essentially all its territory west of the Elbe, and, with it, most of her universities: Duisburg, Munster, Erlangen, Göttingen and Halle all fell under French control. Only the universities of Königsberg and Frankfurt an der Oder remained. A third university was desperately needed to replace those lost. All agreed it would have to be established in Berlin, and Beyme considered setting up the new Berlin institution a 'matter of highest necessity'.[9]

The situation was most galling for Halle. Napoleon took possession of the town (and its university) shortly after his victory at Jena. At first, Napoleon decreed that he would allow the university to continue its activities unmolested. But this was not to last. The Emperor, apparently fearing rebellion from the students, soon ordered the university to close and the students dispersed. Many of the principal professors also left. After Napoleon installed his brother Jerome as King of Westphalia, the university was reopened. But some faculty members refused to return and considered those who did traitors. King Jerome had a sumptuous ceremony to reopen the university, but it was a vain show indeed; Berlin was now more than ever the focus of German intellectual life.

What was to be done with the Halle professors who left out of a newfound loyalty to the German fatherland? They knew that a university or some kind of institution of higher learning would have to be set up in Berlin. But they had no interest in Beyme's dream of an entirely new kind of institution. Instead, they tried to put pressure on the King to transfer all of Halle's assets to Berlin and re-establish the University of Halle, complete with its old professoriate, in the Prussian capital. Beyme, Fichte and others fought this plan since it would (in their view) repeat the errors of the past and close the door on a unique opportunity to change forever academic life in Germany.

In August 1807, the King finally granted an audience to representatives of the Halle community. He was tactful, yet firm: he would not transfer the assets of the University of Halle to Berlin since this could lead to complications with the Kingdom of Westphalia.[10] One must realize that the King's options were limited since French troops remained on Prussian soil and even in Berlin itself. But the King was concerned with more than placating Napoleon's brother. Beyme was, by this time, the King's favourite, and the King seemed well-disposed towards his ideas. In September, the King commissioned Beyme to establish an entirely new university in Berlin. Six members of the Halle faculty were tentatively named for positions at this new institution; some of the remainder returned to Halle in despair.

Beyme demonstrated considerable vision in thinking about how the new institution should be organized. As mentioned above, he favoured some of Schiller's notions of a *Bildungsanstalt*, a teaching institution where great minds could be cultivated. He shrank away even from the term 'university'. But he was not a man of independent action.[11] Instead of moving quickly on the matter, he did little except solicit the views of others. He asked noted scholars to contribute proposals about the new institution. Of all of these, the suggestions by Friedrich August Wolf, J. G. Fichte and Friedrich Schleiermacher were the most influential.

Wolf prepared his response hastily. He had been one of the star professors at Halle, and, like Heyne before him, was that university's leading philologist. His proposal reflected much of Beyme's thinking. Wolf argued that only the best of Halle's faculty should come to the new university – including Heyne himself as master of the philology seminar. Other talented people already in Berlin could be brought in, along with over 120 *Privatdozenten*.[12] Like Fichte, he wished to break German universities out of the narrow pre-professionalism of the past. He complained that students lacked good work habits (*Fleiss*), and that

> Most of them see their studies as a job, and have no greater goal then to get a civil service position through the customary examinations.[13]

Wolf, however, was not popular. His arrogance won him few friends and some falsely accused him of collaborating with the French.[14] He undermined his reputation even more when he broke a promise of secrecy he had given Beyme and presented a copy of his educational plan to a newspaper, which published it.[15] Fichte expressed outrage at this, and, in the meantime, carefully prepared a plan of his own in response to Beyme's request.

The length and exactitude of Fichte's proposal (entitled 'A Deduced Plan for an Institution of Higher Learning to be Established in Berlin') shows that Fichte had not been idle between 1797 and 1807.[16] After leaving his troubles at Jena behind him in 1799, Fichte had moved to Berlin where he began giving private lectures. Eventually he was brought into the Prussian service by Beyme, but he still could not have earned much money.[17] He also took on some teaching responsibilities at the University of Erlangen and rose to the rank of professor in 1805.[18]

As the years passed, Fichte spent more and more time in Berlin, where Beyme and other Prussian officials attended his lectures.[19] It must have been a tenuous existence, since Erlangen is a long way from Berlin, and Fichte by now had a family to support. But Berlin increasingly was where the best minds lived, and there, with informal reading societies (*Lesengesellschaften*) and private lectures, a thriving intellectual community had developed – one that lived outside the traditional university environment. Helmut Schelsky, in *Einsamkeit und Freiheit*, argues that this free, unstructured (though marginal) existence contributed to Fichte's subsequent thinking about higher education.[20] Fichte had of course emphasized the freedom and independence of the scholar years earlier while at Jena, so the concept of *Bildung*, the self-development of the mind, was not new to Fichte. What was very new, though, was his increasing emphasis on nationalism. This shift first appears in a work which Fichte wrote after being named professor of philosophy at Erlangen, a work which shows in a rough form many of the concepts which Fichte used when discussing the University of Berlin.

This work, called 'Ideas for the Inner Organization of the University of Erlangen', was composed in the winter of 1805–6, but not published until well after his death.[21] It clearly reflected his dissatisfaction with German academic life in the wake of the Jena débâcle. He began by arguing the existing universities were worthless, for

> The normal practice at all academies makes the academies completely unnecessary and destroys their essence.[22]

This 'normal practice' consisted of professors droning on and repeating what students could read for themselves. This denied the 'essence' of the university by ignoring the Idea behind the institution, which was teaching 'the ART of the practice of scientific (*Wissenschaftlich*) understanding'.[23] The rest of the work was dedicated to how one could teach this art.

To Fichte, the university remained primarily a teaching institution. Teaching would none the less be tied to the advancement of human knowledge. Fichte advocated the publication of an annual yearbook containing articles on the advancement of knowledge in all subjects. Even students could publish if their work were excellent. The yearbook, argued Fichte, would help foster intellectual competition throughout Germany. This would lead to the progress of human knowledge and further excellence in teaching.[24]

Fichte also recalled an educational experiment which he conducted at Jena. At the end of his course there, he asked each student to write an essay on the difference between *Recht* and *Moral* (roughly, between *lex* and *ius*). He received fifteen essays, of which one stood out for its 'precision, determined and living diction, its deep and original subject' and which was 'without a slavish dependence on my lectures'.[25] Fichte planned to publish this work (much as he now proposed the publication of student essays) but was dismissed from Jena before he could do so.

Fichte had such faith in using the yearbook to foster excellence that he argued that one's career should depend on it. He proposed that a competition be held among faculty members at Erlangen. For one year, each could foster the academic abilities of their students. Their students could then submit articles to the yearbook for competitive review. If any professor failed to produce at least one student whose work merited inclusion in the yearbook, that professor would be denied a permanent place on the faculty.[26] 'Teach well or perish' would be the motto, and Fichte dreamed of thereby turning Erlangen into a *Professorseminarium* (a seminary of professorship).[27]

In some ways, then, Fichte wished to expand upon what he had attempted at Jena. As at Jena, Fichte advocated the development of the students' minds by encouraging young scholars to think both well and independently. He retained his exalted sense of the scholar's importance and the vital nature of the scholar's vocation. But to these ideas he added a new concept: national education. While at Jena, Fichte always saw himself as an internationalist, as one helping to bring on a new age of knowledge and truth for the entire human race. But in the Erlangen plan, Fichte replaced this internationalism with a new sense of Germany's unique importance.

Though Fichte as yet did not dream of a politically united Germany, he did envisage a Germany united by culture. He advocated breaking down provincial barriers by bringing students away from their homes to study. This would expose them to Germans from all quarters and bring out the best in them.[28] All restrictions on study in other states would have to be lifted. Prussia (through Erlangen) could lead the way, but would have to foster competition among all German universities. This would enable German universities to serve the German nation better, since all German universities

> Must not be hindered by externals from drawing forth every talent, cultivating it, and being cultivated by it.[29]

Each province indeed has its own customs and culture. But only by breaking down provincial barriers and allowing students to see people from other areas could a real consciousness of these differences develop. A *'vaterländliches Universität'* so composed could lead to a knowledge of 'German customs and the German national character'.[30] This would lead to patriotism; not a foolish 'Spartanism', but a 'clear patriotism which joins itself with a sense of world citizenship and of German nationhood'.[31] Fichte related all this to his Jena experience, arguing that the rudiments of this process had already begun there before the decline of that university after his dismissal.

So even before the invasion of Germany, Fichte's thinking on universities was closely linked to nationalism, the stepchild of Romanticism. He already saw universities as a means of giving Germany an awareness of its own spirit and of its cultural identity. These ideas were only accentuated and encouraged by the developments of 1806–7.

When Napoleon invaded Prussia, Fichte sought refuge in the easternmost region of the kingdom and removed himself to Königsberg. The King and his court, meanwhile, sought refuge in Memel (a town north of Königsberg). When Fichte returned to Berlin in August 1807, he found a city still occupied by French troops. He none the less fulfilled Beyme's request for suggestions about a new University of Berlin. In fact, the new misfortunes gave him a sense of urgency. Like many others, Fichte was shocked at the impotence of Prussia in the face of the Napoleonic conquest. Something was missing, not just from the court or from the army, but from the nation at large. This need could be fulfilled by a new type of foundation. Over the course of the next year, Fichte described his vision for this institution in his *Deducirte Plan einer zu Berlin zu errichtenden höheren Lehranstalt* (Deduced Plan for a New Institution of Higher Learning, to be Established in Berlin) and his famous *Reden an die deutsche Nation* (Addresses to the German Nation).

One should first note the title of the *Deducirter Plan*. It was 'deduced', deduced, that is, from Fichte's own brand of idealism. And it was not a plan for a university, but, to be literal, 'an institution (*Anstalt*) of higher teaching'. Fichte envisaged starting up an entirely new sort of institution in Berlin, one based on the principles of idealist philosophy and whose curriculum, student body and faculty would differ radically from those in existing German universities.

The Idea behind this institution would reflect Fichte's thought and personality. Instead of creating *Brotgelehrten*, this new establishment would make 'Artists of learning'; it would be a 'school of the art of the scientific realm of understanding'.[32] Previous institutions, with the lowly title of 'university', had merely transmitted existing knowledge without examining it critically.[33] This new school, in contrast, would teach 'the art of critical thought'.[34] It would combine the teaching work of the old universities with the research work of the Berlin Academy. The school would not accept memories from the past, but would examine everything in the critical, dialectical fashion which Fichte expounded in his *Wissenschaftlehre*. It would always question existing knowledge so that the sum of knowledge would grow. And it would expect all students and teachers to do the same, so that they, too, as individuals, could grow and develop.

Everything in the institution – curriculum, faculty, salaries, student lodgings – would be designed towards creating artists of knowledge. Great care would be given to the moral development of students. This would not take place through fear, but by creating an atmosphere where students would train themselves to will the good, and do it:

> The development of the love of honour and the feeling for the sublime as the true vehicle of the moral development of the young must be cared for by teaching and example.[35]

Fichte's language here is striking. Though he was a philosopher and wrote constantly about *Wissenschaft*, here he discusses feeling, and even the sublime, as means to the ends of education. Whether one could call him a 'Romantic' is doubtful, but he had evidently been among them for too long at Jena for their terminology (at least) to fail to have an impact on him.

Fichte did admit that some transmission of mere information would be necessary. There would be 'encyclopaedic lectures' much like those at ordinary universities.[36] But these would be given in the first year only; after that, students who demonstrated promise could enter the real, creative aspects of study in the 'scientific school of art'.[37]

The philosophical faculty would dominate throughout the process. The old upper faculties would fall away or become subservient to the philosophical one. Medicine, for example, would be taught at another type of institution, for Fichte considered it too lacking in *Wissenschaft*, in pure knowledge, to merit a place in his *Anstalt*.[38] Instead of medicine, natural science would take a permanent place in the curriculum, under the aegis of the philosophical faculty. Likewise, jurisprudence would be replaced by history, and theology by historical philology. The philosophical faculty would encompass everything worthy of the name *Wissenschaft*, to the exclusion of all else.[39]

All teaching methods and pedagogy would be dedicated to forming a new kind of fully developed, free-thinking mind. Lectures would not merely repeat what already existed in books, but point out where they were in error.[40] Fichte wished that his methods of teaching, stressing critical thought, creative argument and freedom, should permeate all aspects of the academic process. Examinations and written assignments would reward pioneering thought and comprehension of philosophical principles. Finally, each student would have to complete a masterpiece, in his weakest subject area, to qualify for a degree.[41]

Those who thereby demonstrated a true mastery of scholarship would be granted an entirely new degree: Master of Art (artis magister). Fichte stressed that this must not be confused with a traditional Master of Arts (magister artium), for, he argued, there is ultimately only one art, the art of idealistic philosophy which underlay all academic endeavour.[42] The real masters, the faculty members and scholars of the future, would bear the title 'Master'; those who failed to demonstrate a true comprehension of philosophy would be granted the old-fashioned title of 'Doctor' as a consolation.[43]

These proposals were quite radical, but Fichte's plans for student life were even more so. Fichte never abandoned his dream of making students more moral. In his plan, Fichte envisaged students who devoted themselves entirely to scholarship. He repeated his demand that students study far from their homes to break down their provincialism; attachment to one's home town would be unworthy of a 'man of science, to whom befits a free view exalted above time and place'.[44] Fichte even went so far as to advocate closing other universities in Prussia and using their resources to support the new *Anstalt* in Berlin.[45] He would join these resources with those of the Berlin Academy to support this new institution.

Once they came to Berlin, students would wear uniforms and live together in accommodation run by the school. Some students would live on their own; however, those who lived under the guidance of the State (the 'regulars') would receive preferential treatment. The State would see to the material needs of the regulars; in return, they would be expected to dedicate themselves heart and soul to scholarship. By seeing to their needs, the State would discourage study motivated by material interest and encourage learning for its own sake.

Fichte even prepared an elaborate scheme for financial support. The *Anstalt* would establish a board of elders (mainly *emeriti*) who would receive detailed financial statements from the families of students and then decide what portion of the tuition these families would pay. Truly needy students would have a portion or even all their tuition fees waived.[46] This assistance would be granted as an act not of charity, but of patriotism. For the sake of the fatherland, argued Fichte, no talented youth would ever be turned away because of need.[47] Only regulars would be eligible for this assistance. Fichte even expressed concern that students would lie to get more money and advocated stringent accounting to prevent this.

One should recall that Fichte (like Kant and Schiller) was of humble origin. German universities must already have been open to needy but talented students, and these institutions were certainly not as discriminatory against students from the lower ranks as were Oxford and Cambridge. Fichte sought to make this welcoming of all classes a permanent, regular feature of German academic life. (His financial aid scheme – and the reasoning behind it – is remarkably similar to that in use in present-day colleges and universities in the United States.)

Fichte had high expectations of the faculty who were to teach these students. To help young men become 'artists of knowledge', the new *Anstalt* would need teachers who could 'themselves engage in philosophy as an art'.[48] They must love their art, for

> Nothing yields greater enjoyment than the feeling of freedom and well-directed alertness of the spirit.[49]

And they must have self-consciousness, an awareness of who they are and how this relates to their *Wissenschaft*.

Fichte realized that this programme would demand a great deal of the faculty. He planned to have them be both researchers and teachers, but not at the same time. Active work with students, he argued, would require the energy of young minds. Provisions would be made for older scholars to leave teaching behind after years of service and dedicate themselves entirely to scholarship. They could form a literary society of their own, and, in an atmosphere of complete freedom, go into regions of their respective *Wissenschaften* far beyond those accessible to one burdened with teaching.[50] The older scholars could also take on the administrative work of the institution.

Fichte thus envisaged a scholar going through three phases of life: as a learner, a teacher and finally a 'practising scientific artist'.[51] In all phases, the emphasis would be on intellectual freedom, understanding of philosophical principles and an artistic zeal for knowledge. An *Anstalt* based on these principles would take into itself the freedom and zeal which Fichte found around him at Jena and in the literary societies of Berlin; it would institutionalize this atmosphere so that the young could be fostered in it and join it.

But the proposals to achieve this end were extremely radical. Some had argued for closing Halle or eliminating fraternities, but only Fichte advocated closing all Prussian universities and starting anew.[52] He had no concern whatsoever for the needs of the displaced Halle scholars. Instead, he saw the crisis of his day as a unique opportunity to establish an entirely new kind of institution to provide a new kind of education which would bring about a new kind of Germany.

Nowhere did Fichte make the tie between academic and national renewal clearer than in his *Reden an die deutsche Nation* (Addresses to the German Nation). Given in Berlin in the winter of 1807–8, they called for a national revival even while French troops continued to occupy the Prussian capital. The Addresses discussed all aspects of education, from primary schools to advanced scholarship, but tied it all to a renewal of the German spirit as informed by Fichte's idealistic philosophy.

Perhaps the most distinctive concept of Fichte's philosophy is the 'self-positing I', the 'I' which determines its own existence in an *a priori* fashion. Fichte also presents this as the foundation of education:

> All education strives towards bringing forth a solid, determined, persevering Being, that is no longer becoming but is, and can be nothing other than it is.[53]

To do so, education must not merely train the mind in worldly things, but develop a sense for the eternal.

Fichte even went so far as to prescribe how this development should take place. Students must learn, in early youth, not to see things in nature merely as they are, but to associate them with the underlying laws which control them.[54] After gaining an understanding of the laws of nature, students turn to the 'law of the spiritual nature of man [which is] always and without exception in force'.[55] Once entering this realm of spiritual laws, the students could feel free to reveal their artistic sides. They 'should not at all disdain a poetic excursion into the ideal world, for by nature a light sense for the ephemeral lives with him, he keeps for developing freedom'.[56] The student thereby attains a new kind of knowledge, different from that of the past. It is a knowledge which is 'truthful, sublime beyond all experience, super-sensual'.[57]

But this spiritual education has a higher goal: moral education. The student is a 'work of art', and the process of education is an art with moral results.[58] The student is lifted beyond the physical to the spiritual and, finally, to the moral. He finally learns that he is himself a part of a chain of divine revelation; this knowledge will, in time, lead to the forging of a new, true religion.[59] This new spiritual and moral being would also develop a new sense of devotion to those around him and, in particular, to his fatherland.[60]

Fichte thus saw education as the means to a moral regeneration of Germany. Germany's moral weakness, he believed, made it possible for Napoleon to make quick work of the Prussian army. Fichte, in his *Addresses to the German Nation*, applied this Idea of moral regeneration to all ranks of education, from primary schools to the new *Lehranstalt* which he proposed for Berlin. The result, he hoped, would be a 'new education', which would be 'not the education of a particular class, but of a nation'.[61] Not all would be educated as scholars. Some would become labourers, but they would none the less have access to a primary education. Scholars would be an elite, an elite not of economic or social rank, but of moral perfection born of knowledge. They would lead; the rest would follow.[62] Their excellence would permeate all aspects of national life and revive the German spirit.

Fichte's scholarly elite would form a body very reminiscent of Coleridge's clerisy, albeit in a secularized form. Like the Cambridge Apostles and Cardinal Newman, Fichte saw the scholar serving a moral role which was the real justification for his intellectual one. But the critical difference was that, to Fichte, the instrument used to establish this elite would be not the Church, but the State. Universities had for centuries been state institutions in Germany, and that was one aspect of university life which would remain the same.

Otherwise, Fichte offered the most challenging and radical response to Beyme's call for suggestions for a new university. Fichte would create an entirely new institution with an entirely new purpose: leading the complete moral renewal of Germany. Despite Fichte's protestation that his was a 'deduced' plan and a rational one, the plan was replete with romantic fancy and romantic language. The force of Fichte's personality came through as he called for education in the 'sublime' realm of the 'eternal', and tied all this to German nationalism. The Idea that Fichte had for the new *Anstalt* was as boundless as the sea, but tied (as was so much of German Romanticism) to a growing belief in the greatness of the German *Volk* and the Prussian state.

Not all those from whom Beyme solicited opinions shared in Fichte's dream. Beyme also sought suggestions from Friedrich Schleiermacher, the famed theologian from the University of Halle. Schleiermacher's reply, *Gelegentlichen Gedanken über Universitäten in deutschem Sinn* (Occasional Thoughts on Universities in the German Sense), shows some influence of romantic thought, but differs in many ways from Fichte's proposal. Some have argued that Schleiermacher's work was, in fact, designed as a counter to Fichte's.[63] Whatever his motives were, Schleiermacher presented a plan that was much more conservative in scope than any of the others.

Schleiermacher rejected the plans to create an entirely new type of institution. He made reference to plans for an *Anstalt* in Berlin,

which actually is not university, but which should serve the purpose of a university.[64]

Schleiermacher recognized the radical nature of this proposal, noting that its author wished to destroy the *gotisch Form* of the university and bring about the moral reform of students. But, argued Schleiermacher, the needs of a defeated Prussia did not make allowances for such castles in the air, and he sneered that

he who has leftover time and energy and does not have important things to play with may dare such things.[65]

Schleiermacher then went on to propose that a new institution be created in Berlin, but that it bear the name 'university' and retain the best of what had preceded it.

There were some things which the new university would dispense with. The dominance of the upper faculties would end, and the philosophical faculty would reign supreme. The walls of provincialism, of each little state using universities solely for its own narrow interests, would give way to real academic competition between states and in the pursuit of excellence.[66] Schleiermacher agreed with Fichte that the two universities which remained in Prussian hands were totally inadequate owing not just to their size, but also to their provincialism. So a new institution would have to be founded in Berlin, one that could arouse 'the idea of discernment, the highest consciousness of reason'.[67] This sounds idealistic enough. In fact, one could argue that Schleiermacher had much the same view of the Idea, the purpose, of the university as did Fichte, Schiller and others. But he placed much greater restrictions on the extent to which this Idea should actually dominate academic life.

Schleiermacher, among other things, did not share Fichte's fascination with the State. Fichte envisaged universities as state institutions, and saw no conflict between the interests of the university and those of the State. After all, the State, to Fichte, represented the embodiment of progress and nationalism. Fichte in fact came to believe in a kind of state socialism. Universities (or, rather, the new type of *Anstalt*) would be the moral guide for this State. Schleiermacher, in contrast, saw the State as the natural enemy of the university. To Schleiermacher, the State had narrow, practical interests which were at odds with the unlimited nature of *Wissenschaft*.[68] Schleiermacher admitted that state funds were needed to run universities, but was uncomfortable with this. Above all else, he feared state interference in university work, seeing it as a threat to the free exchange of ideas needed among scholars.

Schleiermacher also had no desire to tie together the university and the academy, and, in the process, create a new type of institution. He saw that there were three kinds of institutions of knowledge: schools, universities and academies. Schools taught mere facts and skills, while academies dealt with the minutiae of *wissenschaftlich* knowledge and left scholars free of teaching responsibilities. Schleiermacher admitted that only a few such academies actually existed, one of which was the one in Berlin.[69] Between the two lay the university, which introduced students to the general spirit which underlay knowledge. It should not be fused with the academy as Fichte recommended, but left alone to continue with its own tradition.

It is perhaps in his vision of student life that Schleiermacher differed most from Fichte. Fichte envisaged a Spartan environment of uniforms and meals in common which would develop the moral as well as the intellectual life of the students. There would be no fraternities, no duelling, no drunkenness, no whoring and no pranks. Schleiermacher, in contrast, argued that students should not be so controlled, but left more to their own devices:

> Should the building of character progress as does the spirit of knowledge, so should the youth become acquainted with the measure and proportion of their tastes. He must thus have freedom in his expenditures.[70]

Schleiermacher defended the traditional fraternities as necessary stepping stones between life at home and an independent existence.[71] While he would perhaps have preferred the university as the gathering place for a few excellent students (as Fichte envisaged it), Schleiermacher argued that allowances had to be made for students of many backgrounds; he went so far as to say:

> It is unavoidable that many come to university who really are not fit for the sciences in the highest sense.[72]

Schleiermacher did not want to change the university, but only to improve it. He wished to keep old forms, but to breath new life into them. He shared in the desire to make young minds great and make universities centres of *Wissenschaft*. But as a career Halle man, Schleiermacher had no desire to overturn all which had come before. Unlike Fichte, he had enjoyed a comfortable academic career with wide acceptance from his peers; perhaps he had too much to lose to take the romantic Idea of a university to the extremes which Fichte did. But the ultimate choice over what form the University of Berlin would take was not in their hands, and, ultimately, not in Beyme's. Owing to political shifts in the Prussian court, Beyme would lose influence soon after receiving the reports he had solicited. When the new institution was actually founded in 1809, it was primarily the work of another man: Wilhelm von Humboldt.

The name of von Humboldt, like those of Stein and Hardenberg, is closely associated with the era of reform in Prussia, an era that helped bring about the rise of the modern German state. Born in 1767, von Humboldt came from a long line of civil servants and army officers. His younger brother, Alexander, won great fame as a scientist on both sides of the Atlantic. Wilhelm's training, however, was mostly in classical languages and antiquities. In 1788, he went to the University of Göttingen where he attended Heyne's seminar in classical philology. Humboldt also encountered Kant's *Critique of Pure Reason*; the resulting combination of devotion to classical studies and to the new idealist philosophy would stay with him throughout his life.

Von Humboldt, however, did not stay in Göttingen to graduate, for his travels took him to two vital cities of the day: Paris and Jena. He went to both at very auspicious times. He visited Paris in July 1789, when the revolution was fresh, new and as yet relatively free of gratuitous bloodshed. His sojourn in Jena came five years later and lasted through most of 1794–6. Von Humboldt was thus there when Fichte enjoyed his greatest prominence. Moreover he came to know Schiller and Goethe, both of whom exerted a considerable influence on his later thought. Like Goethe, von Humboldt travelled to Rome, and found new life in a city that brought him into direct contact with surviving products of the ancient mind. He served as a Prussian diplomatic representative to the Vatican, but managed to find the time to continue studying the ancient Greeks. He hired another German, F. G. Welcher, to tutor his children; von Humboldt none the less took upon himself the task of teaching his eldest daughter Greek.[73]

Von Humboldt became attached to the city and wished to remain there indefinitely. However, events, would force him to leave after Prussia's military defeat, and in 1808 (with considerable reluctance) he began the journey northwards. On his way, he received word that the King had an important new task waiting for him in Prussia.

The new offer came about due to political changes in the Prussian court. After the defeat at Jena, Frederick Wilhelm III desperately sought someone to put Prussia's house in order. The task was staggering. The treaty of Tilsit imposed a sizeable indemnity on Prussia, yet the Prussian King still needed to maintain his army in the hope of reconquering his lost provinces. Both the King and his wife realized that their only hope lay with Heinrich Friedrich Karl vom und zum Stein, a brilliant though somewhat tactless aristocrat and courtier whom the King had dismissed in a fit of pique early in 1807. By August of the same year, Stein was recalled to duty and served the King as prime minister in all but name until November 1808.

One of Stein's first acts was to eliminate his only real rival for the King's ear, Beyme. All contact with the King was made through Beyme; and since Stein despised the man, such an arrangement was unacceptable to him. Stein demanded direct access to His Majesty. To make this possible, the King moved his former favourite out of the executive hierarchy of his government and made him president of the supreme court. Beyme thereafter resigned.

Stein now had exclusive control of the Prussian government and could put his own stamp on it. He later wrote that the 'chief idea' of his ministry was 'to arouse a moral, religious, and patriotic spirit in the nation' so as to enable Prussia to regain her independence and lost domains.[74] Stein took immediate steps, including massive cuts in court spending, to keep the royal treasury solvent. He is, however, best remembered for his long-term reforms, including the rationalization of Prussian government, the abolition of serfdom, and for hiring the man who actually founded the University of Berlin.

Stein's role in the creation of this university grew out of his desire to reorganize the Prussian government and to make Prussia strong again. He divided the government into six main sections, one of which was the section for *Kultus und Unterricht* (religion and instruction). It is interesting to note that Stein, a pious Lutheran, could not resist putting religion and education together in the same section. Von Humboldt, however, would be given no religious responsibilities; these went to someone else. So when Stein recalled von Humboldt from Rome, the latter took on strictly educational duties as director of education.

Von Humboldt received the summons to return to Prussia in late autumn 1808; at this point, he knew he must return, but did not know why. Not until he reached Munich did he discover what his task would be. He was shocked by the news and almost refused the post. Only after he was reassured that he could eventually resume duties in the foreign service (giving him hopes of returning to Rome) did he accept the position.[75] Von Humboldt finally joined the court (then in exile in Königsberg) early in 1809.[76]

At, first, von Humboldt expressed some reservations about the scheme to open a new university. In May 1809 he wrote to Schleiermacher:

I am, as you know, always in favor of the Berlin University, but only because Halle has been lost.[77]

A quick, sudden change in educational practice did not suit von Humboldt. He believed, moreover, that a large capital, expressions all the vices of urban life, would not be a suitable place for the young. If a new university were to be established, von Humboldt would prefer that it be in a quieter place.[78] He did devote some energy to the two existing universities still in Prussian hands. He allocated more money for Königsberg and set up an observatory there. He also took some funds from other sources (including Halle's endowment) and gave them to the University of Frankfurt an der Oder; he then moved this institution to Breslau.[79]

Yet the Berlin project still stands out as the main achievement of von Humboldt's life. Others had dreamed about establishing this institution, discussed it in treatises and gathered together proposals, but von Humboldt was the one who brought the university into existence. Why, despite his hesitancy, was he the one? Part of the answer to this question, of course, lay in timing. Prussia needed a new university now more than ever. But part of the reason also lay in von Humboldt's sympathies with the romantic Idea of a university.

Von Humboldt shared in the romantic fascination with *Bildung*, the self-development of man. He had expressed interest in this concept as far back as 1793, when he wrote a brief piece entitled 'Theorie der Bildung des Menschen' (Theory of Human Education). Von Humboldt argued in this piece that

> the final task of our existence [is]to give to the conception of humanity in our person as much content as possible.[80]

Moreover, he stated that one should study and interact with the world,

> Not so much to become acquainted with it on all sides, but rather to strengthen through this variety the view of our own indwelling strength.[81]

Influenced by Schiller, von Humboldt saw one of the main means to this self-awareness in the study of classical literature. Like Schiller, von Humboldt saw the ancients as fully developed and whole people; by studying their writings, modern man could also aim for establishing his own complete *Menschheit*, his humanity.[82] But since von Humboldt believed in developing all aspects of the human person, he advocated study of other areas, including history and languages.[83]

Von Humboldt retained this broad view of education when he wrote his final outline of the University of Berlin. At the same time (May 1809) that he was expressing reservations to Schleiermacher, von Humboldt penned sketches for the university, which he later presented to the King. Von Humboldt urged the King to see the founding of a new university as an opportunity to regain prestige lost in the French defeat.[84] It is important to note that von Humboldt used the term *Universität* rather than *Lehranstalt*. 'To found a teaching institution,' he argued,

> which was not a university would be, no matter how tempting the thought of newness and the ease of implementation makes it, a mistake, since the concept of such an institution is not even determined . . .[85]

The *Lehranstalt* of Fichte and Beyme now became the *Universität* of von Humboldt, but many of the underlying goals (including *Bildung* and the restoration of national pride) remained.

Besides these theoretical considerations, von Humboldt gave some thought to the financing of the university. One thing he needed to do was work out salary arrangements for some of the more famous scholars he wished to attract. F. A. Wolf was the man he wanted most. Wolf was famed as the organizer of Halle's classics curriculum and as the heir to Heyne's philosophy seminar. Wolf was, as ever, aware of his fame; he demanded 3,000 thaler a year. Von Humboldt, with his special affinity for classical studies, thought he deserved it.[86] Even though von Humboldt was somewhat cool to Fichte, he asked the King to provide Fichte with 800 thaler a year, starting at once, in order to keep Fichte in Berlin until the university was founded. Fichte, who now drew no university income, was in desperate need of the money; illness had kept him from lecturing on his own.[87]

Von Humboldt also gave consideration to the overall financial structure of the university. He firmly believed the university would make the German nation stronger. State funds would clearly be needed to establish it. Von Humboldt, however, expressed concern over possible state interference in academic affairs. As a result, he wanted the university to establish an endowment of its own, which would eventually give it some financial independence from the state.[88] He did not share Fichte's vision of direct state control since he was far more fearful than Fichte of the possible consequences this could have for academic freedom and the free, unfettered spirit of *Wissenschaft*.

On 24 July 1809, von Humboldt presented his final version of this proposal to the King. He estimated that, at least in the beginning, the university would require 150,000 thaler per annum to function. The King accepted the proposal. A commission was soon thereafter established to gather together faculty for the institution. Karl Gauss, the famed mathematician, was offered 1,500 thaler; Fichte (who had been drawing 800) would now receive 2,000. Humboldt knew that Fichte could be difficult and so wanted him to draw a good salary.[89] Schleiermacher also agreed to join the faculty.

Some time after taking these substantial steps towards getting the university started (instruction did not begin until the autumn of 1810), von Humboldt prepared a detailed sketch of the theory and organization of the university. This work, entitled 'Über die innere und äussere Organization der wissenschaftlichen höheren Anstalten in Berlin' (On the Inner and Outer Organization of the Higher Scientific Institutions in Berlin), did not appear in print in his lifetime. It is undated, though it apparently dates from late 1809 or early 1810. It represents a culmination of thought about how the University of Berlin should function, and what Idea lay behind it.

Von Humboldt did indeed use the term *Anstalt* here; however, it soon becomes clear that he was primarily discussing the new university in Berlin. In von Humboldt's scheme the academy would still exist. But no academy had, in his estimation, excelled in recent times, and had had little real place in the advancement of *Wissenschaft*.[90] The academy, then, should be tied to the university and they should have members in common. Von Humboldt thus adopted some of Fichte's proposals; he kept the academy as a place for research unfettered by teaching responsibilities, but did not specify that it should be reserved for retired scholars. The academy did in fact lose its independence in September 1809; together with some museums in Berlin, it was put under direct state control.[91] The university thus became the centre of focus for his essay and his term in office.

Like his romantic predecessors, von Humboldt stressed the ethical and national importance of the university. The new institution in Berlin would be, according to von Humboldt, the 'pinnacle' for the 'moral culture of the nation'.[92] It would join 'objective *Wissenschaft*' with 'subjective *Bildung*', thereby making both the individual and the state strong.[93] The *Wissenschaft* would have to be 'pure', free from the limitations of short-term need; only if the scholar enjoyed 'isolation and freedom' could the purity of scholarship be maintained.[94] 'If one fails,' maintained von Humboldt,

> to seek knowledge or develop himself . . . everything is irretrievable and forever lost, lost for science . . . and lost for the state.[95]

Von Humboldt thus declared that both teaching and research should take place, or, rather, teaching through research. He saw no inherent conflict between the two; in fact, he believed that teaching would stimulate *Wissenschaft*. Students and faculty members would enjoy a special relationship based on equality. Both would pursue *Wissenschaft*; this pursuit would be the means to *Bildung*.

This model is reminiscent of Fichte's ideas.[96] Fichte wanted students to act like young scholars in their own right, publishing papers and developing keen arguments in colloquia. Humboldt took some of these ideas and worked to put them into an institution with the traditional name of 'university'. Helmut Schelsky, in *Einsamkeit und Freiheit* (Isolation and Freedom) argues that von Humboldt's dream of students learning through practising pure *Wissenschaft* became the ideal for all subsequent German universities. He admits, however, that later generations became distracted from this ideal. It also been argued that due to von Humboldt's influence, *Bildung* became subordinated to *Wissenschaft*, and that teaching, especially undergraduate teaching, has as a result suffered in Germany ever since. Certainly Fichte's attention to teaching was lost and the hierarchical, professor-oriented German university was now looming.

Von Humboldt, so honoured in German academic circles, ironically never presided over a functioning university. He always wanted to return to the foreign service; in August 1810 he did so, accepting a post as ambassador to Vienna. The first lectures at the new University of Berlin, a university populated by the leading names in German academics, began a month later.

# 5
# Cambridge and Oxford, 1830–50

As Stephen Prickett argues, Romanticism became a part of the early Victorian intellectual world, a world otherwise dominated by utilitarianism. Wordsworth and Coleridge were particularly influential in the university environment, while Lord Byron had a larger popular following. The Lake District poets formed the heart of a 'minority tradition' of philosophy, theology, aesthetics and ethics which informed many in the Oxbridge world with a special sense of purpose.[1] For a time (especially in the 1830s and 1840s) the followers of Wordsworth and Coleridge held considerable influence in the Oxbridge world. Their thoughts, combined with the revival of religiosity felt through much of the early Victorian world, presented a strong, well-articulated counterweight to the principle of utility.

Though Coleridge did not present a blueprint for university structures and curricula, his works provided principles which guided many in the next generation at Cambridge. An education so guided would be at once elitist, philosophical and literary. It would be elitist, in that it would be designed to cultivate a small group as the moral guide for the nation. It would be philosophical, in that it would combine thinking about the nature of knowledge and truth with the Anglican tradition. And it would be literary – not so much because Coleridge and Wordsworth prescribed this, as because the poetical works of these men and of the other Romantics would be held in high regard by a generation steeped in their philosophy.

The best place for such an education was the college. The colleges had always been elitist, for even the largest, Trinity, had a manageable number of students. They had close ties with the Church of England, in that they owned clerical livings in the country and required their masters and other senior dons to be in holy orders.

And since they taught and did not examine for degrees, they could (and did) allow students to read outside the standard curriculum of mathematics and classics. From the 1820s onwards, this flexibility opened the door for literary and philosophical studies.

Of all Cambridge's colleges, one that clearly demonstrated the impact of the romantic Idea of a university was Trinity. Trinity occupied a leading position among the colleges, and the others tended to follow Trinity or St. John's in political and educational matters. It was the largest and most well-endowed of these institutions. It was also an academic powerhouse, and especially showed its strength by dominating the classical tripos examination for decades after the first such competition held in 1824.

Romanticism's impact at Trinity had ramifications for the whole university. People such as the Apostles, Julius Hare and William Whewell formed a Coleridgean clerisy of sorts at Trinity, a clerisy that sought to guide the college, the university and the nation.

Trinity's clerisy consisted of several small groups of men who by word and deed showed a dedication to the romantic Idea of a university. At the core of these groups lay the Cambridge Apostles, an undergraduate society founded in 1820. This organization was one of several begun in this era; it soon became the most famous, and it has the special distinction of still being in existence.[2]

The Apostles' main purpose was educational. As one of its early members observed years later, the society was based on 'a belief that we *can* learn, and a determination that we *will* learn, from people of the most opposite opinions'.[3] The society stressed freedom of thought, invoking a 'spirit of the pursuit of truth with absolute devotion and unreserve'.[4] The Apostles sought to expand on the university experience by meeting informally outside the confines of the university structure. Undergraduates ran it, and a few figures came to emerge by the late 1820s as first among equals. Some of these played a key role in defending Cambridge from the onslaught of utilitarianism, and used concepts taken from Wordsworth and Coleridge to do so.

One of the leaders of the early Apostles was Arthur Hallam. Hallam came up to Cambridge in 1828 and was made an Apostle the following year. He was very enthusiastic about the Romantics; he once wrote to a friend in regret that 'I tried to convert the nicest woman on earth to Wordsworth and failed.'[5] Hallam, though, is best remembered not for his life, but for the great elegy written in his honour after his death in 1833 by fellow Apostle, Alfred, Lord Tennyson.

*In Memoriam*, Tennyson's greatest work, is a revealing meditation on Tennyson's state of mind after his friend's death. In one stanza, Tennyson echoes the fears of the Lake Poets that knowledge was becoming worldly and godless. Although he personifies knowledge as a beautiful young lady, Tennyson warns that

> A higher hand must make her mild,
>   If all be not in vain; and guide
>   Her footsteps, moving side by side
> With wisdom, like the younger child:
>   For she is earthly of the mind,
>   But wisdom heavenly of the soul.

Stanza CXIV

Tennyson elsewhere tied his fear of godless, heartless education directly to Cambridge:

> Therefore your Halls, your ancient Colleges,
> Your Portals statued with old kings and queens,
> Your gardens, myriad-volumed libraries
> Wax-lighted chapels, and rich carven screens
> Your doctors, your proctors, and your deans
> Shall not avail you, when the Day-beam sports
> New-risen o'er awakened Albion-No!
> . . .
> Because the lips of little children preach
> Against you, you that do profess to teach
> And teach us nothing, feeding not the heart.[6]

Like Wordsworth, Tennyson saw the child as a 'mighty prophet/ Seer blest', a pure being whose voice spoke with more authority than all the scholars. Tennyson, moreover, inherited Wordsworth's dread of universities which 'fed not the heart' and failed to serve the soul of men.

Yet for all the admiration expressed for Wordsworth, it was Coleridge who chiefly dominated the Apostles and helped shape their approach to higher education. Coleridge lived until 1834; his final years were spent at his home in Highgate, in London, welcoming a train of admirers. His close proximity to Cambridge (as opposed to Wordsworth's distant residence in the Lake District) may help explain Coleridge's impact. Carlyle, who was by no means one of Coleridge's disciples, said of him:

> he had, especially among young inquiring men, a higher than literary, a kind of prophetic or magical charm.[7]

F. W. Maurice was one of several Apostles who frequented Coleridge's home and adopted many of his ideas. Maurice shared Coleridge's vision of renewing English society by reviving the minds of the young. John Kemble echoed these sentiments and applied them specifically to educational institutions:

> All reform is misplaced which does not begin by reforming our system of education, from the lowest to the highest and from the dome school to the university. . . . Education must be taken out of the hands of the parsons, till the parsons are educated for their tasks of educating others. The clerisy of the land must no longer be the parsonry of the land.[8]

Coleridge's vision of Cambridge as a training ground for the clerisy which would serve as a moral rudder for the nation thus took root among the Apostles.

Maurice promoted this vision as an alternative to the utilitarian ethos. In his later life, Maurice complained that when he came to Cambridge, 'among the younger and cleverer undergraduates of the day, especially in Trinity, Benthamism was the prevalent faith'.[9] Maurice countered this faith with an emphasis on the moral development of students and chastised the public for wanting universities to send students 'into the market neat, showy, and saleable' and for crying to the universities:

> Grind, hammer, and weave away! We want graduates made to sell; and if the universities will not supply us fast enough, we must reform them.[10]

Maurice resisted this external pressure to reform Cambridge by defending the curriculum then in use with its emphasis on classics and mathematics.[11] To Maurice, previous efforts to change it had led only to the institution of new examinations (such as the classical tripos introduced in 1822) which led to empty 'cramming', leaving students with an 'outward, produceable, dead, unconnected, atomic kind of knowledge rather than that which is living, harmonious, and profound'.[12]

Maurice, like Coleridge, saw knowledge as a breathing, living, organic whole which could feed the moral as well as the intellectual aspects of students. In his eyes, new examinations, new curricula and new educational nostrums would not bring about this education. Only a strong relationship between teachers and students could do so:

> nothing in all probability can remedy this but the more liberal and constant communication between the minds of the teachers and the taught, and above all, the strong resolution on the part of the former to consider and sympathize with the individuals they are instructing.[13]

Maurice, Kemble and other leading young men among the Apostles wanted to make universities better, not by changing their outer structures but by revitalizing the educational process within this structure. They did not call for the abolition of colleges, the addition of new, more rigorous examinations, or the professionalization of the teacher. After all, Cambridge's structure gave them the time and freedom to take their educations largely into their own hands. Colleges were the appropriate venue for this type of education, and having taken advantage of the collegiate system, the Apostles showed no desire to eliminate it. Their point of view was shared by two fellows at Trinity, and, eventually, by the head of the college himself.

One of the fellows who shared this vision was Julius Hare, who came up with William Whewell in 1812 and remained a close friend of Whewell's for the rest of his life. Hare was a fellow from 1818 until he left to take a clerical living in 1832. For decades thereafter he corresponded with Whewell. This correspondence gave him ample opportunity to express his thoughts about education; moreover, it illustrates both the aspirations Romantics had for Cambridge and the impossibility of fully realizing these dreams.

That Hare was a friend of Romanticism cannot be disputed. After he joined Whewell and Wordsworth for a walking tour of the Lake District in 1844, Hare described the vistas seen there in the lushest romantic terms.[14] He was openly hostile to empiricism, arguing, in a youthful letter to Whewell, that 'Plato is worth ten thousand Aristotles and 1,000,000,000 . . . Lockes.'[15] Years later, Hare congratulated Whewell for denying empiricism and for being 'so zealous and vigorous in maintaining the contrary truth'.[16]

Hare's embrace of Romanticism led him, over the years, to advise Whewell on educational matters; taken as a whole, these admonitions show in detail what Romantics expected of universities. Like Coleridge, Hare argued that to 'educate' meant to 'bring out that which is in man'.[17] How could a curriculum do this? By having, Hare argued, religion and philosophy at its centre.[18] Hare joined vehemently in the growing chorus against Paley, noting the 'pernicious influence of our teaching Paley on the morals of the country' and telling Whewell that

> it would be a great thing to substitute [Chambers'] evidences for Paley's; a Christian life breathes from *his*, and would pass into the hearts of many.[19]

To Hare, another impediment to developing young minds was some of the very reforms undertaken since 1800 to improve the university, especially the addition of new competitive examinations. In 1841, Hare quoted his friend Maurice as saying that adding a divinity tripos 'would surely be an abomination'. Hare strongly agreed with this, arguing that 'emulation has done enough harm already'. He then looked back warmly to the previous century, when knowledge was pursued, he claims, 'for its own sake . . . and not for the prizes attached to it'.[20] Two years later, Hare argued that Oxford was surpassing Cambridge, and that 'we shall continue to sink, unless we get rid of our system of drilling for parade and of our morbid stimulants, and adapt a system which will call forth a living power and train our students to walk without leading strings'.[21]

This statement, of course, begs the question of how such a system could be established. When Hare accepted a lectureship at Trinity, he clearly took the task seriously, calling it a 'tremendous undertaking, and attended with an overwhelming responsibility, to have to teach the flower of England's youth to walk straight in these crooked-going days'.[22] Hare clearly had no faith in institutional structures such as examinations for this task. Instead, he repeatedly told Whewell that the only thing of real value was direct teacher-to-student communication. He wrote to Whewell in 1841:

> the only truly powerful influence, by which men's minds and characters are lastingly affected, is personal, that of mind on mind, of moral character on moral character. The advantage of institutions seems rather to be that of affording facilities for such influence, and of keeping it within legitimate bounds.[23]

Hare voiced almost identical sentiments in 1844, arguing that the 'personal influence' of a gifted man was 'of far greater importance than anything than mere institutions can effect for the development and cultivation of all life, especially religious life'.[24]

Hare thus saw the college teacher functioning in a pastoral role. He was to be a moral shepherd to his students, but to lead mostly by presenting an example. While no high churchman himself, Hare could not help but admire the example the leaders of the Oxford Movement set for their charges. 'What a mighty power,' he wrote, 'has been exercised of late years at Oxford by Newman and Pusey . . .'[25]

Over the course of more than twenty years, then, Hare advocated the Coleridgean Idea of a university. Here would be a place where philosophy and religion would be the core of studies, and one in which the latent faculties of young men would be cultivated with pastoral care and personal concern. How could one ensure, though, that tutors are Newmans, Puseys or Maurices and not dry-as-dust pedants? How, to paraphrase Max Weber, could the charisma of a great teacher be institutionalized and routinized? For much of this time, moreover, Hare was speaking to Whewell not as a direct participant in university affairs, but as an interested bystander. Whewell, in contrast, was involved in college and university affairs throughout his entire adult life. A test of how influential the romantic Idea of a university was at Cambridge is thus to be found in his story.

Whewell was a giant at Cambridge. Though the son of a craftsman, his brilliance gained him an entrée to the elitist world of Cambridge and eventually made him its dominant figure. The breadth of his competence was truly amazing; among his respected publications were works in theology, the theory and practice of education, applied science and the philosophy of science.[26] He served as Master of Trinity for over twenty years (1841–66) and as the university's vice-chancellor in 1842–43. Given his prestige as a scholar and his lofty collegiate position, he was certainly the strongest individual to be reckoned with at Cambridge in the 1850s and 1860s.

There is not doubt as to Whewell's power and influence; it is, however, more difficult to discern his relationship with Romanticism. Like Coleridge and his friend Hare, Whewell was, to some extent, enamoured of things German. He travelled to the Harz Mountain region in 1825.[27] Two years later, with Hare he planned another journey to Germany. Whewell finally had to beg off, but he suggested they travel instead to a domestic pilgrimage site for Romantics: Tintern Abbey.[28]

Whewell maintained a long friendship with William Wordsworth. On several occasions, Wordsworth wrote remarkably frank letters to Whewell concerning Cambridge affairs, including one on Catholic emancipation and the admission of dissenters to degrees.[29] Whewell joined in Hare's North Country wanderings with the poet in 1844, and, the following year, Whewell dedicated his *Elements of Moral Theology* to Wordsworth, a dedication which Wordsworth acknowledged with appreciation.[30]

In addition to his friendship with Wordsworth, Whewell demonstrated admiration for other Romantics. He joined Hare in a fruitless effort to establish a prize in Christian philosophy in Coleridge's name after the poet died in 1834. Whewell himself expressed admiration of Coleridge's thought, but was concerned that some at Trinity did not appreciate Coleridge's philosophy and tended to remember only his erratic personal life.[31] Whewell also obtained for Trinity the statue of Byron that still looms large in the Wren library and later acquired a bust of Tennyson as well.[32]

Whewell joined the Lake Poets in presenting the Church of England as a vital weapon in the fight against liberalism. He strongly believed religion was a part of education, and considered it necessary 'in saving something from the barbarizing and selfish tendency of vanity and luxury'.[33]

It is true that Whewell perhaps was best described as a broad churchman. He did, after all, support a grace to admit dissenters while he was vice-chancellor.[34] He nevertheless also supported mandatory chapel, and his correspondence, philosophical works and even scientific writings (such as his *Bridgewater Treatises*) all bespeak of a sincere dedication to the Church of England and a strong desire to keep Cambridge tied to it.[35] This reflected the Burkean, organic view of universities common among the Romantics.

Whewell's attachment to this conservative view of how universities were run was made clear by the role he played in several controversies Cambridge faced during his tenure as Trinity's Master. These struggles with external critics of the university and with commissions charged with investigating or changing it forced him to reveal what he believed about the university. These struggles were the chief means by which the romantic Idea of a university helped shape Cambridge's destiny even into the twentieth century.

The first struggle arose from Whewell's disagreement with Charles

Lyell, the most famous English geologist of the mid-nineteenth century. In 1845, Lyell published an assault on Oxbridge in his *Travel in America*. Lyell argued that the old, classically-oriented curriculum failed to promote the sciences, and that German-style research professorships should replace the colleges and their tutors. To achieve this, Lyell joined those who called for a royal commission to reform the universities, break down the colleges and crush 'the power and *vis inertiae*' of these 'forty learned corporations'.[36] Though Lyell was hardly the first to attack the colleges, his voice was a famous and loud one, and the drive to reform the universities from without was gaining steam.

Whewell's response, couched in Coleridgean language, was that the universities were already performing their function well and that changes imposed upon them from the outside would do more harm than good. According to Whewell, the main purpose behind education was to develop the innate faculties of the mind, faculties that he called 'Ideas'.[37] Furthermore, Whewell, like Coleridge, believed in the need to balance ways from the past with new innovations. In his *On the Constitution of Church and State*, Coleridge had argued that the learned clerisy was needed to keep the 'permanent' aspects of society, those represented by the landed elites and their culture, as a balance to the potentially overwhelming force of the 'progressive' culture of the industrialists. Whewell applied this same dualism to the university curriculum. 'Permanent studies,' Whewell argued,

> are fitted to educe two principle Faculties of man considered as an intellectual being: namely, language and reason.

The permanent aspect of education was, to Whewell, the most important, as it gave young minds the foundation they needed to understand the world.[38] Whewell associated these permanent studies with the traditional Cambridge curriculum of classics and mathematics.

Whewell believed that the system of colleges worked best to teach these core subjects. The close interaction between tutor and student made the students an active participant in the educational process. The traditional 'college' lecture, consisting of a student reading and translating a classical text with close guidance from the tutor, was, to Whewell, superior to the passive experience of the 'university' or 'professorial' lecture featured at German universities, which was a speech in front of a large group. To Whewell, the professorial lecture was best reserved for the 'progressive' aspects of the curriculum, new or specialized areas of knowledge which were less important to the essential job of developing the minds of the young. To eliminate the college, as Lyell advocated, would be to take away the heart of education.

Like Burke's society, Whewell's university was connected to generations past, present and future. The permanent studies, including the traditional texts by Homer, Virgil and Euclid served as glue to hold the tradition together. And, like Coleridge, Wordsworth and the Apostles, Whewell believed that developing the minds of the young should take priority over research into new areas.

Whewell defended this position when encountering what he considered a much more menacing opponent: the royal commission of 1850. After years of pressure from utilitarians, the government finally called for a royal commission to investigate how to improve Cambridge. The university was, of course, aghast at this and the Senate informed the Prince Consort, then Chancellor of the university, that this commission 'must be regarded as intended to promote an ulterior motive' and spoke at length of the threat it posed to the liberties of the university.[39] Albert responded that the commission was inevitable and that dons had best cooperate with it in order to avoid further arousing the university's enemies.[40] The commission thereafter set to work.

Like many of his colleagues, Whewell clearly disliked the commission and considered it a dangerous intrusion into university affairs. He agreed to cooperate with it, but argued it had no right to compel evidence, and insisted all its work be done in writing; which it was. Though many dons refused to give evidence to the commission at all, Whewell did. His evidence (and his testy relationship with the commission) demonstrate his attachment to Cambridge as he knew it.

Whewell's main concern was to defend the collegiate system. He did not consider professors any replacement for tutors and the close methods of the tutorial system. Though an admirer of things German, he had no taste for German-style *Lernfreiheit*. He went so far as to say, 'mere private preparations for examinations, with or without private tutors, cannot with any propriety be called teaching.'[41] As in the past, Whewell stood by the colleges because they offered direct and interpersonal instruction.

As a man notorious for his occasional outbursts of temper, Whewell was probably overreacting to the commission, for in preaching the gospel of traditional education to it, he may have been preaching to the choir. The commissioners included the Bishop of Chester, the Dean of Ely, Sir John Romilly and Whewell's old friend Adam Sedgwick. Of these men, two were high-ranking Anglican clerics, and a third, Sedgwick, was, like Whewell, a scientist who in the past had vigorously defended the traditions of Oxbridge. In its final report, the commission did not advocate any major changes in the tutorial system or the colleges, and noted that

> what above all other things gives us hope for the future good of Cambridge is the manly, free, and truth-loving character of her sons, springing in part, at least, from her collegiate system.[42]

The commission's outlook was, overall, conservative. It did not seek to remake the university radically, but only to make what changes were absolutely necessary. Near the conclusion of its report, it argued that

> in proposing reforms, we do not wish to dissociate the present from the past; neither do we recommend changes except for the purpose of removing positive evils.[43]

It was not this commission which really offered a threat to the Anglican, collegiate and tutorial-oriented Cambridge Whewell had always known. Most of its recommendations for changes were modest: there should be a slight expansion of professorial offerings; several new honours triposes should be established; and fellowships and scholarship should be offered on a more open basis. Whewell himself had promoted similar gradualist reforms. He took his Knightbridge Professorship of Moral Theology far more seriously than did his predecessors and gave regular lectures on this topic. He successfully created two new triposes for Moral and Natural Science. Whewell's view of the university did not rule out change, but insisted that it be natural and not forced upon it by outside interests.

But change from the outside was indeed coming. In response to the royal commission's report, Parliament, in 1856, passed the Cambridge University Bill to review and change the statutes of the university and its colleges. As these statutes dated back to Elizabethan times, this had the potential to mark a fundamental change in direction for Cambridge. The new law established a commission (commonly known as the Statutory Commission) to renew these statutes. Colleges were required to submit new statutes by 1 January 1858. To create these statutes, the law did not recognize the traditional college leadership of the Master and senior fellows; instead, the Master had to gain the consent of *all* fellows (whether in residence or not) before he could pass along the college's own revision of its statutes to the commission.[44] If the college failed to present satisfactory revisions by the specified date, the commission had the right to impose revisions on the college which could only be blocked by a two-thirds plurality of fellows.[45]

Late in 1857, the commissioners presented some 'general principles' which it hoped the colleges would adhere to in revising their statutes. It advocated allowing laymen to be Masters of colleges, opening up all college scholarships and fellowships to free competition, and sharing collegiate wealth with the university in order to improve professorial lectures. These proposals went beyond the first commission's recommendations and would secularize the university, lessen the importance of the colleges and encourage professorial as opposed to tutorial instruction.

Whewell responded to this commission with far more vehemence than he did the previous one. He clearly resented the coercive powers which this commission could invoke to change college statutes. In January 1858, Whewell presented a pamphlet dedicated to the issues raised by the commission which represented one of his last major public statements about the Idea of a university.[46] Whewell clearly objected here to the wholesale revision of collegiate statutes. 'Constitutions are not made, but grow,' he argued, for

> we can no more sweep away an old living institution and immediately put a new one to live in its place, than we can cut down a forest of oak and forthwith have standing on the same ground a grove of firs.[47]

Whewell thereupon rehearses familiar arguments for retaining the collegiate system unchanged. To him, 'college teaching, with the close contact into which it brings teachers and pupils, and the pupils with one another, appears to be full of advantages which no other system can compensate.'[48] As in his *Liberal Education*, Whewell again argued that collegiate instruction is best suited for the general education required during the first two years of study, after which time more specialized instruction could take place using the professorial method. Given his desire to defend colleges, Whewell also expressed concern about attempts to use collegiate wealth to fund professorships.[49]

Whewell was most vehement about leaving the roles of Masters and fellows as they were. In a pamphlet released a few weeks earlier, Whewell strongly opposed admitting laymen to the office of Master. Given the college's role 'in the moral and religious education of the country', Whewell wanted Masters to be in orders.[50] Here one certainly hears echos of Coleridge's clerisy. Whewell also strongly argued against opening up fellowships to university-wide competition, for it would create a situation where even a strong fellow would become a non-resident, feeling 'no tie to college duties' and tending 'after having gained one step in the career of life in this way, [to] go and seek elsewhere in some professional or literary career which removes him from the university'.[51] The result, Whewell feared, would be that 'instead of literary and scientific men, we should have persons with the attainments of clever and well-taught schoolboys'.[52] Whewell was aware that the process of professionalization described by Sheldon Rothblatt in *The Revolution of the Dons* had begun. Opening up competition for fellowships to all, regardless of their college, would encourage this process. But Whewell, with his belief in the need for a 'philosophical character' among the dons, had no desire to participate in this revolution. He did not see dons as secularized professionals placed into the narrow boxes of disciplines; they were still, in his eyes, to be men of broad learning, good character and godliness.

Whewell's spirited defence of the colleges and his politicking among the fellows did have some effect. The first draft of statutes presented by the commission in May of 1858 included most of the proposals which Whewell considered objectionable, including lay masters and complete free competition for fellowships. After Whewell galvanized the opposition to these proposals, they were modified. The next drafts of a year later required that Masters be in holy orders, kept celibacy for most fellows and made the opening of fellowships optional.[53] Whewell forestalled, but could not stop the revolution of the dons. After his death in 1866, Cambridge would see the professionalization and secularization of its faculty.

The situation Whewell faced late in his life reflects the difficulties inherent in trying to make the romantic Idea of a university a reality. In his letters to Whewell, Julius Hare had the luxury of discussing this Idea in the abstract. Unlike Whewell, Hare did not, after 1834, have to deal with the realities of bickering dons and extramural pressures to make Trinity and Cambridge more utilitarian. And, while Whewell himself clearly did heed some of Hare's advice and his Coleridgean view of how a university should be run, he by no means accepted all of it. Despite Hare's objections, Whewell promoted the new tripos examinations to encourage competition among the undergraduates. While Whewell believed a university should be the moral rudder of the nation, he could not accept that its colleges should permit the kind of unguided self-development promoted by the Apostles. To Whewell, education in college was an ordered, hierarchical process. He argued in 1834:

> our colleges have employed, most happily, I think, and wisely, the force of method and habit of authority and prescription, in short, of system and discipline.[54]

This discipline required fellows and tutors to be in control. As Whewell most pointedly put it, the university was *not* a place 'where a man may educate himself, and where the students, by their social intercourse, may enlarge and cultivate each other's minds'.[55]

But Whewell, by adopting some of the beliefs of Wordsworth, Coleridge, the Apostles and Hare, did revive Cambridge's spirits in the early and mid-nineteenth century and help preserve many of its institutions into the twentieth. Thanks in no small part to him, the university retains its collegiate structure and its emphasis on tutorial instruction for its undergraduates. It remains one of the great academic hubs of English life; if anything, Cambridge plays a larger role in the intellectual life of the country now than it did in the eighteenth century. The same is true of Oxford, which was likewise revived by the coming of the romantic Idea of a university.

As at Cambridge, this Idea came through a small band of dedicated students and teachers chiefly from one of the university's colleges. Prominent members of this group came to be associated with the university as a whole, which thus gave the Oxford Movement its name and a notoriety in society at large greater than that of the Cambridge Apostles and their allies.

Oriel College, the birthplace of the Oxford Movement, stood out from the other Oxford colleges even before the Movement began. It was the only college which awarded fellowships on merit alone, and in fact had instituted by the 1820s a rigorous system of competitive examinations for prospective fellows. As a result, serious scholars tended to collect there, coveting the distinction of having won an Oriel fellowship and enjoying some of the most intellectually stimulating company the university could offer. The college's provost, Edward Copleston, had surrounded himself with fellows, including Thomas Arnold (later the famed Headmaster of Rugby), John Keble (a famed churchman) and, eventually, Edward Pusey and John Henry Newman.

Copleston's followers, known as the 'noetics', turned away from the style of life which had typified the Oxford fellow in the past century. The wine bottle gave way to the teapot; Socratic, dialectical arguments in the common room and a serious dedication to scholarly responsibilities became the norm.[56] These efforts seem to have improved the moral climate of the college; Samuel Wilberforce, then a student and son of the famous anti-slavery advocate, wrote to his sister:

> At Oriel there are not perhaps about two or three men whom you can call really religious, a great proportion of moral, hopeful, *good sort* of men, and on the other hand men occasionally perhaps actually immoral but who would not obtrude their actions and dispositions on their acquaintances ...[57]

This account differs significantly from those of Gibbon and his contemporaries; moreover, Samuel Wilberforce was a child of a religious family who himself later became a staunch bastion of the Anglican Church, particularly in it conflicts with Darwinism. Clearly, something had changed.

The noetics were concerned more with debate and clean living than with strenuous intellectualizing. As A. Dwight Culler says, 'they reasoned more than they read'.[58] They displayed little knowledge of Continental philosophy; it was said, for example, that only two men in the entire university could read German; neither was at Oriel.[59]

But their example inspired other colleges to emulate Oriel. By 1830, Balliol came to be regarded as a rival to Oriel. When years later Thomas Arnold sent his own son, Matthew, to Oxford, the young man went to Balliol. At Christ Church, meanwhile, several men who would later achieve fame were getting their educations, including William E. Gladstone and Edward Pusey. In the university as a whole, it was becoming less fashionable, at least in some circles, to spend vacations carousing in London; instead, reading parties were sponsored which brought friends together to continue their education.[60] Through the 1820s, however, Oriel remained the pre-eminent college of Oxford and provided the atmosphere in which the Oxford Movement came into being.

The one Oriel fellow and tutor who more than anyone presaged the Oxford Movement was John Keble. Keble, named fellow in 1811 and tutor in 1817, brought with him many of the traits later characteristic of Newman, Pusey and others. Like them, he was a high churchman with a good mind and a serious attachment to the Christian faith. His devotional work, *The Christian Year* (1827), became one of the most influential books of its day among religious students and scholars at Oxford. Keble, moreover, was keenly aware of the spiritual value of Romantic poetry. He spent his undergraduate days at Corpus Christi College, where John Taylor Coleridge, a nephew of the poet, introduced him to the works of William Wordsworth. Keble thereafter developed a strong admiration for Wordsworth's poetry.[61]

Keble also shared in the romantic tendency to see all knowledge as belonging to an interconnected web of truth held together by the Creator. He was one of only a handful of men to gain First Honours in both mathematics and classics, demonstrating a profound master of both the major subject areas then in the Oxford curriculum.[62] Like nature itself, the university, believed Keble, did not educate minds by writing on a Lockean *tabula rasa*, but by cultivating innate faculties of the mind.[63] The mind grew organically, as did the Church (at least in its Apostolic forms, which included the Roman, Eastern and Anglican communions), and society as a whole.[64] As with Coleridge before him and Newman afterwards, Keble tied his educational ideal to the gradual moral development of society, a development to be guided by the Church.

The Oxford Movement which Keble presaged and helped begin was thus an educational *cum* religious phenomenon. It shared in many aspect of the romantic Idea of a university, with its emphasis on serious learning for its own sake and education as a means to a better society. But even more than the Cambridge Apostles, it members gave a religious articulation to these goals. In many respects they completed a process begun by Coleridge, one of taking German thoughts about education and informing them with religious ardour.

The two leaders of this Movement both came to Oriel in the early 1820s. John Henry Newman, a Trinity product, won a scholarship as an undergraduate, but did not achieve honours. The competitive examinations for Oriel fellowships gave him another chance to test his mettle; moreover, the good name of this college had won his attention. He won the competition, and came to Oriel as a fellow in 1822. Pusey arrived the following year; the two soon became friends. Newman was ordained in the Church of England in 1825 and took up a post as tutor at Oriel in 1826.

Unlike some at Oxford, Newman took this dual role of priest and tutor very seriously. He agreed with the statutes of Archbishop Laud, which made the tutor a 'moral and religious guardian to the youths committed to him'.[65] The tutor thus had a pastoral responsibility for his students. This concept, while on the statute books, had fallen into complete disuse in the eighteenth century and its revival in the nineteenth was not without difficulty.

Newman faced obstacles from several directions in his attempts to serve as a pastoral tutor. Some students pulled childish pranks on him when he tried to control their nocturnal carousing.[66] Neither of the college provosts under whom he served (Edward Copleston and Edward Hawkins) offered him support. This is somewhat surprising in the case of Copleston, who had some interest in education in the colleges and defended Oxford against assaults in the *Edinburgh Review*. Hawkins in fact opposed Newman's attempt to reform the tutorial system and build closer ties between students and individual tutors.[67] Newman, however, carried out these reforms *de facto* on a personal level, forming close relationships with some of his better students and taking charge of overseeing their moral wellbeing. This was a process reminiscent of Fichte's change from trying reform Jena as a whole to his efforts to contribute to the *Bildung* of his better students through the seminar system.

This pastoral mission was expanded to a national scale with the advent of the Oxford Movement itself. The date traditionally assigned for this was July 1833, when John Keble gave a sermon on national apostasy. 'Reform' was then the word of the day, a word that generally meant utilitarian reform sponsored by the Benthamites in government. To Keble, Newman and Pusey, such reforms (including the elimination of religious tests at the universities or the suppression of church properties) were a threat to the apostolic Church of England. After Keble's sermon, Newman published the first of many 'Tracts for the Times', one which implored the reader to 'CHOOSE YOUR SIDE!':

should the government and the country so far forget their God as to cut off the Church, to deprive it of its temporal honours and substance? . . . I fear we have neglected the real ground on which our authority is built – our APOSTOLICAL DESCENT.[68]

Unlike Whewell, Newman had no desire to allow dissenters into the universities; to do so would in his mind undermine the clerical nature of these institutions. The Church of England was to Newman not a Protestant Church, but an apostolical one with a special mission for the English people. Newman wanted universities to remains part of this Church, albeit one that would serve in their pastoral capacity more completely and vigorously than they had in the past. Above all, Newman wanted to protect the universities from interference by outsiders who would judge good from evil not with godly discernment but by the cold workings of Bentham's hedonic calculus. Pusey shared in these goals and also worked towards their fulfilment.

Newman, however, was not able to stay with his vision of the apostolic Anglican Church forever. He and Pusey began discussions of a revival of monasticism in the Anglican tradition. Newman, meanwhile, dreamed of establishing a college of priests who would serve the needs of some rough industrial city.[69] Pusey did in fact later help establish Anglican convents. Newman, however, eventually came to believe that only the Roman Church was truly apostolic. One of his tracts, 'Tract 90' (1841), tried to demonstrate that many of the Thirty-Nine Articles were not really at variance with Roman Catholic teaching. This led to a storm of protest against the entire Oxford Movement and an end to the writing of tracts by its followers. In the following year, Newman removed himself from university life and formed a small religious community of his own; here, at Littlemore, he was welcomed into the Roman Communion in 1845. Newman did eventually build his urban house of priests. This was the Oratory of Birmingham; the priests there were, of course, Roman Catholic. Newman, meanwhile, had left Oxford in 1846, and was not to see it again from 32 years.

Edward Pusey accompanied Newman part way on this road to Roman Catholicism but stopped short in time to stay in the Church of England. After his election as Tutor at Oriel (1823), Pusey became concerned about the possible impact of the higher criticism which was then becoming popular at German universities. Much of this new criticism came about as techniques in philology developed by Heyne and his successors were applied to Biblical texts.

Pusey feared that Oxford and Cambridge could be overwhelmed by scepticism about the Bible since they were unprepared to counter the force of argument arising from German scholarship. In order to equip English universities against this threat, Pusey, accepting the adage of 'know thy enemy', went to Germany for four months in 1825. He visited the universities of Göttingen and Berlin, met Schleiermacher and got a thorough taste of German scholarly life. He returned the following year to continue his studies of Hebrew and learn Arabic and Chaldaean, neither of which was taught with any seriousness at Oxford. When he returned to Oxford in June of 1827, Pusey had a substantial knowledge of Semitic languages. As a result of this training, Pusey really had mastered his subject when he was named Regius Professor of Hebrew in 1828. The same could not be said of many of his predecessors.

Other things went into the education of this remarkable man as well. While on the Continent, he visited Mont Blanc and thus went on the standard pilgrimage of the sublimity seeker.[70] After his return from Germany, he went north to Derbyshire, staying for a time with Southey, the Coleridge family and Sir Walter Scott.[71] He thus had ample contact with Romantics and their beliefs.

Another great teacher was grief. Pusey, in 1828, married a woman he had loved for years. The marriage was a happy one and resulted in several children whom Pusey (and Newman) cherished. But Pusey's wife died in 1839 after a long illness, and several of their children died afterwards. Pusey was never the same; he took to wearing black, refused to sit for portraits and felt his misfortune was a punishment from God.[72] All these events only increased his religiosity and dedication to the Church of England.

This devotion came to a test when the royal commission came to Oxford as it did to Cambridge in 1850. Pusey, considering the commission illegitimate, refused to testify before it. He instead chose other venues in which to defend the Church of England and the university which he considered a vital part of this Church.

After their investigations were completed, the commissioners proposed limiting clerical control and a shift in power away from the colleges and towards the central body of the university. They believed that Oxford was behind foreign (especially German) universities in research in the natural sciences. Matthew Arnold made a similar observation in 1874, and wrote:

It is in science that we have most need to borrow from the German universities. The French universities have no liberty, and the English universities have no science; the German universities have both.[73]

To combat this deficiency, the commission proposed taking some students out of the jurisdiction of the colleges and putting them under the direct control of professors.[74] Needless to say, the colleges (and their Masters) were not pleased with this proposal when it was published in 1852. At Oxford Pusey became one of their spokesman; in 1854, he published *Collegiate and Professorial Teaching and Discipline* to combat these innovations.

Pusey directly attacked the commission's call to elevate the professor. Professorial lectures, as practised in Germany, seemed to Pusey to be educationally useless. Pusey argued that German professors tended merely to dictate to their students, and that students would be better served by reading books about the subjects under discussion.[75] Besides, a lecture was a one-way conversation. It imparted information in a passive fashion without developing the mind of the hearer.[76] There was no opportunity for dialogue, conversation and direct interaction between student and teacher.

For Pusey, a worse problem was the failure to develop the independence of mind of the student. Students became too dependent on the lecturers.[77] German professors did not produce fully developed minds, but slavish disciples. Locke, for instance, left no school behind him in England, but in Germany 'Wolf, Kant, Fichte, Schelling, Hegel, exercised by turns an almost undisputed sway'.[78]

Pusey blamed this tendency to imitate squarely on the dominance of the professor. He emphasized that his problem was not with professors in and of themselves, but with 'the idolatry of the professoriate'.[79] Pusey noted that

The first oriental professors in Germany, and I believe in France also, taught catechetically in their private lectures – the very lectures which most aided the pupil.[80]

One is reminded of Heyne's seminars or Fichte's *conservatoria*. In the decades following Fichte's death, German universities and their professors had indeed become famous; there may well have been some truth, though, in Pusey's argument that in making professors great, the German system made students small.

Worst of all, argued Pusey, professors in Germany failed to see to the moral welfare of students. Professors in both countries had long since abdicated this responsibility, but there were no colleges in the German system to take up this work in their stead. The result, argued Pusey, was inattention to public worship, duelling and brawls.[81] Here again it should be noted that Fichte and other Germans influenced by the romantic Idea of a university had also voiced concerns over the behaviour of students. If Pusey's observations of German academic life in the decades after Fichte are correct, it casts doubt on how much real success Fichte and other had in their endeavours.

But there was a principal difference between Fichte or other German reformers and Pusey. Pusey did not call for *Bildung durch Wissenschaft*, or education through the advancement of science. 'The main object of the university,' argued Pusey, 'must be the cultivation, not of science, but of men.'[82] And this cultivation was not to glorify man, but God:

> History, without God, is a chaos without design; political economy without God would be a selfish teaching about the acquisition of wealth. . . . Even the intellect cannot be cultivated aright, unless it be subdued to God, and its whole cultivation be in reference to Him.[83]

The best means to do this was to preserve the college with its tutors and fellows where instruction could be combined with careful guidance. The tutor met his students regularly and had direct contact with them in small numbers. Tutors, moreover, were (at least in theory) in residence. The result of this personalized, supervised instruction was, to Pusey, a superior cultivation of the whole man. 'I see no good reason,' he argued,

> why Oxford and Cambridge should throw aside their sober, methodical lore for the unchastened speculations of Jena or Berlin. If those universities are fertile in books, we by God's blessing at any rate bring forth men.[84]

An affirmation of these ideas came from the pen of Pusey's sometime colleague, Newman. Even though Newman left Oxford and the Anglican Church in 1845, he remained a defender of Oxford's structure. The same beliefs which took him to Roman Catholicism also made him a conservative in higher education. His position on these matters, so well articulated in *The Idea of a University* (1852), represents a culmination of his experience in the Oxford Movement and a clear expression of the romantic Idea of university.

The fundamental concept which led Newman to Catholicism appeared in 1843 in the last sermon he gave at Oxford. Newman published this work two years later as his *Essay on the Development of Christian Doctrine*. The theory of development which this work discussed was important both in his own life and in his view of the world around him. Through the acceptance of the Christian religion, argued Newman, a real incremental change took place. The believer grew to a better, more perfect understanding of himself and of God; through this, he became a better person.

There was nothing shockingly new here, except in the way Newman came to apply this belief. As development and growth took place on an individual level, so, too, did it in society and the Church. This argument convinced Newman that he could overcome the last remaining stumbling blocks to his crossing over to Catholicism, including the acceptance of Catholic Mariology and the authority of the papacy. These doctrines clearly were not Biblical, nor were they explicitly discussed in the writings of early Fathers of the Church. They were consequently unacceptable to any Anglican, for, as Article VI of the Thirty-Nine Articles states:

> Holy Scripture containeth all things necessary to salvation: so that whatsoever is not read therein nor may be proved thereby is not to be required of any man that it should be believed as an article of Faith, or be thought requisite or necessary to salvation.

Newman, however, now accepted the Roman Catholic doctrine of a continuing historical revelation. To the Roman communion, Scripture and the primitive church are not a sufficient guide, for the will of God is continuously revealed through the teaching authority of the Church in history. Change takes place, in a gradual, evolutionary, tradition-oriented way. Christ, for example, gave the keys of his Kingdom to St. Peter (Matthew 16:19); subsequently, the see which St. Peter established assumed a position of vital and finally pre-eminent authority within the Church. The seed of truth established in the Gospel, therefore, grew into the institution of the papacy; during Newman's own lifetime, this authority was reinforced with the recognition of papal infallibility at the First Vatican

Council, a council which thereby validated a concept which had been discussed within Catholicism for centuries.

Newman likewise saw an historical development in his own life and thought.[85] His conversion to Christianity came when he was fifteen. Long before he became a Catholic, he decided that he was called to celibacy. As time wore on at Oxford, he became entranced with monasticism as idealized by the Romantics. After crossing over to the Roman communion, Newman considered all of these as steps along the way, showing a gradual development towards his joining the Roman Church. He believed that he himself was gradually guided to truth as was the Church.

This Idea of Development (as Meriol Trevor calls it in his biography of Newman) proved to be key to Newman's Idea of Knowledge and his Idea of a University.[86] 'Self knowledge,' wrote Newman, 'is at the root of all real religious knowledge.'[87] Even after he left Oxford, Newman exhibited a fondness for it and a distrust of for utilitarian reforms. This became clear when he published his justly famous work, *The Idea of a University*, a collection of lectures given after he was named to head the new Catholic university of Dublin. Due to arguments with the Archbishop of Dublin, Newman's tenure as head of this university (1852–8) was not very successful; however, the book which resulted from this assignment was.

Newman made clear from the outset that he considered the university primarily a teaching institution. Its purpose, he argued, was 'the diffusion and extension of knowledge, rather than the advancement'.[88] It was neither an institution for scientific research nor a seminary, but a place where young minds could grow with proper guidance. The university's faculty, moreover, could not be expected to teach and do research all at once:

> To discover and to teach are distinct functions; they are also distinct gifts, and are not commonly found united in the same person. He, too, who spends his day in dispensing his existing knowledge to all comers is unlikely to have either leisure or energy to acquire new.[89]

The dilemma of teaching versus research was, of course, not limited to the Oxbridge system. Newman's solution was to leave teachers to teach, and trust that research would go on outside the university. Fichte would make the scholar a teacher in his prime and a researcher in his age. What in fact largely happened in German universities by the mid-nineteenth century was the sacrifice of teaching for the sake of research, with the professorial lectures and *Privatdozenten* left to take care of teaching the undergraduates. This question remains unresolved in America today, where scholars are expected to do both, but often find that Newman's observation on this matter is all too true.

To Newman, the knowledge thus transmitted was an end in itself. Scholars gathered together to share ideas, and students would also be caught up in the atmosphere. The result was what Newman called a liberal education, one which formed good habits of mind.[90] Newman scoffed at writers in 'a celebrated Northern Review' who wished to tie this education to 'utility', and quipped that 'if a healthy body is good in itself, why is not a healthy intellect?'[91] Newman admired Copleston's earlier efforts in defence of a liberal education and quoted from them at length. Newman did, however, ascribe a social and practical value to liberal education, using an argument still employed by its advocates:

> I say that a cultivated intellect, because it is a good in itself, brings with it a power and a grace to every work and occupation which it undertakes . . .[92]

But unlike some modern proponents of the liberal education, Newman believed that it had some limitations; these shaped his view of what made a university complete.

To Newman, liberal education needed the guidance of religion. It could not in itself make the whole man, for 'liberal education makes not the Christian, not the Catholic, but the gentleman'.[93] Newman retained the pastoral view of education present in his Oxford days. Religion and theology always had a definite role to play, only now the religion would be Catholicism. Religion helped keep young men away from immorality; more importantly, it kept the institution, and, through it, the nation away from apostasy. Newman feared that if theology were not part of the curriculum, secular philosophies would take its place. Science, for example, could set itself up as the 'measure of all things', so, too, could political economy.[94]

Newman, however, had no interest in subsuming science to theology. He wanted to keep science free, but to prevent it from usurping theology's role. He had no need of Paley's natural theology to demonstrate the existence of God, and in fact turned the entire design argument on its head:

I believe in design because I believe in God, not in God because I see design.[95]

There was also no need to trouble undergraduates with these matters either, for 'to have recourse to physics to *make* men religious,' retorted Newman, 'is like recommending a canonry as a cure for gout.'[96]

Newman himself was a man of conscience who suffered dearly as a result; this experience probably gave him sympathy for scientific freedom, and, by extension, for academic freedom. When he left the Anglican Church in 1845, he was forced to leave behind his entire world. He acted as his inner voice demanded. Even after conversion he remained and individualist, and wrote in his *Apologia*:

> If I am obliged to bring religion into after dinner toasts... I shall drink – to the Pope if you please – still to conscience first, and to the Pope afterwards.[97]

One could even argue that by breaking the tie between science and theology (with his denial of the design argument), Newman would leave science freer than it had been in his Oxford days. Science no longer would need to prove anything about God; all it had to do was not pretend that it disproved His existence. After all, the main reason for having theology in the curriculum was pastoral. 'A university,' he wrote in his *Idea*,

> is, according to the usual designation, an Alma Mater, knowing her children one by one, not a foundry, or a mint, or a treadmill.[98]

Newman was fond of his own alma mater, and defended its methods even if he now considered its theology to be in error. 'There is a sort of self-education in the academic institutions of Protestant England', he noted, 'here there is a real teaching.'[99] He strongly defended the colleges where this self-education took place; to him, colleges 'constituted the integrity of a university'.[100] His conservative outlook here clearly reflected how his Idea of a university partook of the Romantic Idea of a university.

Newman divided the roles of university and college in a way which was quite in line with Coleridge's philosophy. Newman had certainly read Coleridge and had some admiration for him. At one point, Newman criticized Coleridge's indulgence in 'liberty of speculation, which no Christian can tolerate'; but went on to praise him for instilling 'a higher philosophy into inquiring minds, than they had hitherto been accustomed to accept'.[101] Like Whewell, Newman adapted Coleridge's distinction between the 'permanent' and the 'progressive' aspect of society to the university situation. The college, Newman argued, served the needs of 'stability', while the university 'embodied the principle of progress'.[102] Colleges were at the heart of the educational process, for they provided 'the formation of character, intellectual and moral, for the cultivation of the mind . . .'[103] Colleges would thus serve the permanent aspects of study, while professors and the university at large would serve the more progressive sciences.

Newman thus joined the defence of the collegiate system with its tutors and its traditional curriculum. Like other Englishmen influenced by the romantic Idea of a university, he saw universities as places designed primarily to cultivate the minds of the young. Like Whewell, Maurice and Pusey, he saw the college as the proper place for this cultivation and the traditional classical curriculum as the appropriate means. He shared in the English tendency to use the romantic Idea of a university to defend what already existed against the growing tide of utilitarianism.

The future, however, did not entirely turn out as these men would have wanted. The royal commissions, long dreaded, came to both universities in 1850 and published their reports several years later. Parliamentary action followed. In 1854, an Act of Parliament declared that no oath need be taken for a degree; all religious tests were dispensed with in 1871. Enrolments thereafter increased dramatically. After 1882, Fellows and tutors no longer had to be celibate. The universities were ceasing to be institutions of the Anglican Church, becoming instead, to some extent, national institutions. The separate and distinct role of the tutor and the professor remains; the colleges still to this day take on the primary responsibility for educating undergraduates, while the university sponsors lectures and laboratories and grants degrees. Oxbridge's Romantic defenders clearly did win some victories in their struggle with the principle of utility; in part because of their efforts, the universities at Oxford and Cambridge today are very different their German counterparts. But what has irrevocably passed is their real, effective tie to the Church of England.

# Epilogue:
# Whither the Romantic Idea of a University?

Were it possible for Fichte, von Humboldt, Whewell or Newman to wander again in the places they helped make great, there would be much that was new to them. Though all these men are revered, much of what they would see, at first glance, would indicate that their spirits (and thoughts) had been absent for many years and that their presence had been reduced to statuary placed in their memory. But has the romantic Idea of a university really gone? And if so, where did it go?

Like many German universities, Jena went through a great transition in the nineteenth century, and was transformed from a small, *kleinstaat* teaching institution into a *Wissenschaftsuniversität*. Fritz Ringer, in his *Decline of the German Mandarins*, provided the English language audience with an insightful analysis of this transformation. Now would come the day of well-paid professors, *Privatdozenten* struggling to earn a chair, ample state support, and constant talk of *Bildung*, *Lernfreiheit* and *Lehrfreiheit*. Ringer argues that these terms, however, had lost the meaning they had acquired in the days of Fichte and had become mere shibboleths. 'The ideas of the Reform period,' says Ringer, 'were gradually routinized and transformed into defense of social privilege.'[1] Jena became particularly noted for its medical faculty, and it was to a Jena clinic that Nietzsche was brought after his descent into complete madness.

In the twentieth century, Jena of course was not spared from the German catastrophe of Nazism and war. As the city of Jena had grown from a small Thuringian town into an industrial centre (including the optical works of Carl Zeiss) it was a target of allied bombing; given the inaccuracy of bombing, it was inevitable that serious damage would befall the university's buildings. After the

134

war, Thuringia (and with it, Weimar and Jena) found itself in the Soviet zone of occupation, thus putting the university under the pall of the Soviet *Weltanschauung* for the next forty years.

The university survived none the less. Renamed the Friedrich Schiller Universität, it celebrated the four hundredth anniversary of its founding in 1958. Letters and dignitaries came from around the communist (and even non-communist) world. As part of this celebration, Professor Max Steinmetz of Jena compiled a monumental history of the university from its founding until his own day.[2] This history, occupying two oversized volumes bound in red cloth, is a remarkable achievement. It of course abounds with some of the Marxist ideology of that era; eighteenth-century student beer riots, for example, become in its pages examples of class struggle. But Professor Steinmetz and his *Dozenten* did their work with Teutonic thoroughness, and the archival resources of the region were picked clean to make this an invaluable effort.

The end of the Soviet era had meant yet another transformation for Jena. FSU (as it is now called) finds itself having to compete for students with universities throughout Germany. Like virtually all of them it relies heavily on state support though it is now opening up to private funding. As housing is reputedly cheaper in the East, many have found Jena attractive and enrolments, now topping 10,000, have doubled since 1989. Jena shows signs of becoming, of all things, more like the 'multiversities' of America. Like its American counterparts, it invests heavily in new building. The Law Faculty is housed in a splendid new building with a fine modern library near the 'Goethe Galleria' shopping mall and a McDonald's. An entirely new faculty, that of the *Wirtschaftswissenschaften* (business sciences) boasts similarly opulent facilities. The very existence of such a faculty would scarcely have been imaginable a few generations ago at a Germany university. So, too, would the curriculums in Sports Science and Media Studies. The Historical Institute, meanwhile, has its offices and library in considerably more modest surroundings, though a new central library is in the works for the philosophical faculty.

None the less many of the hallmarks of the post-von Humboldt *Wissenschaftsuniversität* remain. The university still has no central campus; instead, faculties are scattered around the city. The administration remains limited in size, and students are left to fend for themselves for housing and other necessities. Junior faculty members, unlike the *Privatdozenten* of the past, are paid, but they still show due deference to the professors. The 'political change', the polite term used in the East for the fall of communism and unification, has brought with it a new awareness of markets and of students; nevertheless, Jena remains a research institution like most of its fellow German universities. Like them, it still puts undergraduate teaching below research, valuing von Humboldt's ideal of *Einsamkeit und Freiheit* over Fichte's emphasis on *Bildung*. Surely Fichte would feel lost amidst the conflicting forces at Jena; none the less he remains, along with Schiller and Goethe, a local as well as national hero, and Jena's role in the development of German universities is remembered with pride.

Cambridge University has been spared some of the tumult which Jena has suffered over the past sixty years, and were William Whewell to see it today he would probably feel more at home than his German counterpart. There are, of course, now more colleges than in his time and many more tripos examinations. When Whewell died in 1866, Cambridge had four triposes (two of which he had helped create); now there are 31. The very nature of what a tripos is has changed as well; now, instead of just being an examination offered at the end of one's university career, a tripos is more of a prescribed course of study with several examinations required en route. Julius Hare would of course be aghast at this scenario, but one imagines that Whewell would be more accepting of it. Teaching is now much more specialized and the tendency to divide things into intellectual compartments, already begun by the end of Whewell's life, has continued apace. So has the bureaucracy of instruction, as instructors at Cambridge are now subject to Teaching Quality Assessment in a manner long familiar to American college teachers. But the colleges, the tutorial system and the emphasis on personalized instruction which those influenced by romanticism strove to preserve are still there. So, too, are the King's College Chapel, the backs, and the Wren library at Trinity, complete with the statue of Byron which Whewell helped acquire. One can only guess at his reaction to the much smaller busts of himself and his friend Julius Hare in Trinity's library.

The buildings are there – but what about the Idea beneath them? In 1834, Whewell received an intriguing letter from none other that William Wordsworth. In it, Wordsworth declared that 'the spirit of John Bunyan brushed by me' and related to Whewell the contents of a recent dream. In this dream, wrote Wordsworth, he saw the Cam in flood, a flood so great that it attacked the base of King's College Chapel. 'Out came the Provost, Fellows, and Students,' he

continued, 'and to my great astonishment, fell to work most man-
fully for the destruction of the buttresses.' Members of this crowd
explained to the poet that 'we are pulling them down, that the
flood may have free way.'[3] What was the nature of this flood in
Wordsworth's dream? The flood was the drive to separate the university from the Church of England, for Wordsworth wrote the letter
in opposition to the support offered by Whewell and others to Connop
Thirlwall, whom Wordsworth's brother had deprived of his fellowship for his support of admitting dissenters. Were Whewell to visit
Cambridge today, he would see that this flood has become a tor-
rent. Religious tests disappeared in the late nineteenth century, and
the university now exists to a large extent at the pleasure of a
thoroughly secular state. The influence of the Church of England
has fallen greatly due to the impact of Darwin and the First World
War to the point where one scholar has written seriously about
'post-Christian Britain'.[4] Cambridge – and English society – has not
only ceased being Anglican; it has ceased (in any but the most
limited sense) to be a Christian institution of higher learning. Most
of the English Romantics would certainly disapprove of this development, and perhaps be concerned that the *form* of their Idea
(decentralization, tutorial instruction, etc.) had been preserved
to some extent, but the real *substance* of it had been lost.

One could, however, offer a message of comfort to Fichte, Hare,
and the other figures discussed in this book and send their spirits
back to their hard-earned rest. Much of their best work was done
outside of the established structure of their universities. Fichte's
*conservatoria* were informal meetings centred on a charismatic teacher;
though they have now been routinized into the seminar system,
their spirit still depends on the instructor involved. The tradition
of extracurricular student organization still lives on at Cambridge
and helps stimulate the minds of undergraduates and fellows. The
English and German versions of the romantic Idea of a university
spoke as one about two things: universities should primarily be
about teaching, and great teaching requires the interaction of great
teachers with involved students and involved students with one
another. When seeking to apply the lessons of this era, one must
bear in mind the delicate nature of this business. And above all
follow Hippocrates' dictum: 'First, do no harm.'

# Notes

## Preface

1 Immanuel Kant, *Werke*, vol. 12, *Über Pädagogik* [On Pedagogy] (Frankfurt: Insel Verlag, 1964), 700.
2 Sheldon Rothblatt, 'The Idea of the Idea of a University and its Antithesis', in *Conversazione* (Bundoora, Australia: Latrobe University, 1989), 11.
3 *Ibid.*
4 *Ibid.*, 6.
5 Otto Bollnow, *Die Pädagogik der Deutschen Romantik* [German Romantic Pedagogy] (Stuttgart: W. Kohlhammer Verlag, 1962), 64.

## Chapter 1

1 Novalis, *Hymns to the Night and Other Selected Writings*, trans. Charles E. Passage (Indianapolis: Bobbs Merrill Company, Inc., 1960), 45.
2 Friedrich Paulsen, *Die Deutschen Universitäten und das Universität Studium* [German Universities and German University Study] (Berlin: 1902; reprint Hildesheim: Georg Olms Verlagsbuchhandlung, 1966), 40–52. All citations are to the 1966 edition. Paulsen speaks of the 'territorial-confessional university' of the sixteenth and seventeenth centuries. I have adapted and expanded this concept, speaking in terms of the *purpose* of the university (hence the confessional 'Idea') and applying it to England as well as Germany. For a discussion of the confessional division of Germany, see Ernst Zeeden, *Die Entstehung der Konfessionen* [The Rise of Confessions] (Munich: R. Oldenbourg, 1964).
3 Paulsen, *Deutschen Universitäten*, 38–9.
4 J. D. Michaelis, *Raisonnement Über die Protestantischen Universitäten in Deutschland* [Reasonings over the Protestant Universities in Germany] (Frankfurt and Leipzig: Privately printed, 1768), passim. Michaelis streses the mercantilist advantages of having a university in one's own domain.
5 Paulsen, *Deutschen Universitäten*, 40–1.
6 Paulsen, *The German Universities*, trans. Edward Delavan Perry (New York: Macmillan & Co., 1895), 49.
7 Peter Searby, *A History of Cambridge University, Vol. 3, 1750–1870* (Cambridge: Cambridge University Press, 1997), 12.
8 D. A. Winstanley, *Unreformed Cambridge* (Cambridge: Cambridge University Press, 1935), 302.
9 Charles E. McClelland, *State, Society, and University in Germany, 1700–1914* (Cambridge: Cambridge University Press, 1980), 55.
10 *Ibid.*, 30.
11 Max Steinmetz, ed., *Geschichte der Universität Jena* [History of the University of Jena], vol. 2 (Jena: Fischer Verlag, 1958), 175.
12 Paulsen, *Deutschen Universitäten*, 57.
13 McClelland, 63.

14  *Ibid.*, 211.
15  *Ibid.*, 212.
16  *Ibid.*
17  Ronald Hayman, *Nietzsche, A Critical Biography* (New York: Oxford University Press, 1980), 62.
18  Michaelis, 3.
19  *Ibid.*, 12–13.
20  *Ibid.*, 16–17.
21  Michaelis, 21.
22  *Ibid.*
23  *Ibid.*, 22.
24  *Ibid.*, 87. Cf the debates in the *Berliner Mittwochgesellschaft* (1795) concerning the closure of universities. This salon-like club of Berlin intellectuals and writers saw the universities as an obscurantist waste (McClelland, 77).
25  *Ibid.*, 98.
26  Michaelis, 71.
27  *Ibid.*, 72.
28  *Ibid.*, 74.
29  *Ibid.*, 79–80.
30  *Ibid.*, 91–2.
31  Michaelis, 172.
32  Henry Richards Luard, *Graduati Cantabrigienses* [Graduates of Cambridge] (Cambridge: Cambridge University Press, 1884), 670–1.
33  W. R. Ward, *Georgian Oxford* (Oxford: Clarendon Press, 1958), 129. See also L. S. Sutherland and L. G. Mitchell, eds., *The History of the University of Oxford*, vol. V, *The Eighteenth Century* (Oxford: Clarendon Press, 1986), 212–13.
34  *Ibid.*, 61.
35  Oxford Historical Society, *Brasenose College Register* (Oxford: Clarendon Press, 1909), addendum.
36  Searby, 11.
37  Winstanley, *Unreformed Cambridge*, 41.
38  *Ibid.*, 41–2.
39  *Ibid.*, 47.
40  Searby, 3.
41  Jeremy Bentham, *Works of Bentham*, ed. John Bowring, Vol. 10 (Edinburgh: William Taft, 1843), 37.
42  *Ibid.*, 37.
43  Edward Gibbon, *Autobiographies*, ed. John Murray (London: John Murray, 1896), 59. Note that both Bentham and Gibbon attended Westminster school before going to Oxford; Gibbon had much better things to say about Westminster than about his university.
44  *Ibid.*, 81–4.
45  *Ibid.*, 67.
46  *Ibid.*
47  *Ibid.*, 70.
48  D. B. Horn, *A Short History of the University of Edinburgh* (Edinburgh: Edinburgh University Press, 1967), 40.

49  *Ibid.*, 63.
50  Adam Smith, *An Inquiry into the Nature and Causes of the Wealth of Nations* (New York: The Modern Library, 1937), 717.
51  *Ibid.*, 718.
52  *Ibid.*
53  *Ibid.*, 733.
54  Alfred Body, *John Wesley and Education* (London: The Epworth Press, 1936), 65–6.
55  Robert Southey, *Life of Wesley*, Vol. 1 (New York: Harper and Brothers, 1847), 80.
56  *Ibid.*, 80–2.
57  *Ibid.*, 91.
58  *Ibid.*, 94–5.
59  Body, 101.
60  Vicesimus Knox, *Liberal Education: or, a Practical Treatise on the Methods of Acquiring Useful and Polite Learning*, Vol. 1 (London: Charles Dilly, 1788), xvi.
61  Knox, 1:1–2.
62  *Ibid.*, 3.
63  *Ibid.*, 4.
64  *Ibid.*, 9.
65  *Ibid.*, 98.
66  *Ibid.*, 138.
67  *Ibid.*, 139.
68  *Ibid.*, 108.
69  *Ibid.*, 125.
70  Ward, 72.
71  Winstanley, *Unreformed Cambridge*, 138.
72  Vicesimus Knox, *Liberal Education: or, a Practical Treatise on the Methods of Acquiring Useful and Polite Learning*, vol. 2 (London: Charles Dilly, 1788), 202.
73  Gibbon, 76.
74  Knox, 2:180.
75  *Ibid.*, 181.
76  Sheldon Rothblatt, *Tradition and Change in English Liberal Education* (London: Faber and Faber, 1976), 16.
77  Knox, 2:101.
78  Rothblatt, *Liberal Education*, 32.
79  *Ibid.*, 75.
80  Michaelis, p. 115. Also Knox 2:156.
81  Knox, 2:156.
82  Rothblatt, *Liberal Education*, 123–4.

## Chapter 2

1  W. H. Bruford, *Germany in the Eighteenth Century* (Cambridge: Cambridge University Press, 1968), 236.
2  *Ibid.*, 241–2; Helmut Schelsky, *Einsamkeit und Freiheit* [Solitude and Freedom] (Düsseldorf: Bertelsmann Universitätsverlag, 1971), 18.

3  Frederick Copleston, *A History of Philosophy*, vol. 6, *Wolff to Kant* (Westminster, MD: The Newman Press, 1960), 106.
4  *Ibid.*, 109–10.
5  Schelsky, 19.
6  Copleston, *Wolff to Kant*, 112–13.
7  Bruford, *Eighteenth Century*, 243.
8  Paulsen, Friedrick, *Immanuel Kant*, trans. J. E. Creighton and Albert Lefebvre (New York: Charles Scribner's Sons, 1902), 31.
9  *Ibid.*, 30.
10  *Ibid.*, 32.
11  *Ibid.*, 59–60. These included Mauer's *Theory of Reason*, and Baumgarten's *Metaphysics*.
12  *Ibid.*, 12.
13  Paulsen, *Immanuel Kant*, 111.
14  *Ibid.*, 112; from the 'Architectonics of Pure Reason' section of *The Critique of Pure Reason*. Given Kant's deep and lifelong admiration for Rousseau, the allusion to Rousseau's lawgiver is almost certainly intentional.
15  Immanuel Kant, *The Critique of Pure Reason*, trans. by Norman Kemp Smith (New York: Modern Library, 1958), 10.
16  Paulsen, *Immanuel Kant*, 113; from the 'Architectonics of Pure Reason', in *The Critique of Pure Reason*.
17  Immanuel Kant, *Prolegomena to Any Future Metaphysics*, ed. Lewis White Beck (Indianapolis: Bobbs-Merrill Publishing Co., Inc., 1950), 115.
18  Kant, *Critique of Pure Reason*, 7.
19  Immanuel Kant, *Werke*, vol. 12, *Über Pädagogik* [On Pedagogy] (Frankfurt: Insel Verlag, 1962), 700–1.
20  *Ibid.*
21  *Ibid.*
22  *Ibid.*, 699.
23  *Ibid.*, 698.
24  *Ibid.*, 722.
25  Ernst Cassirer, *Kant's Life and Thought*, trans. by James Hader (New Haven: Yale University Press, 1981), 362.
26  Kant, 12:706.
27  *Ibid.*, 710.
28  *Ibid.*, 710.
29  *Ibid.*, 737.
30  Paulsen, *Immanuel Kant*, 61.
31  Kant, 12:704.
32  Cassirer, 376. According to Ernst Cassirer, Frederick the Great distrusted Wöllner as a 'swindling, scheming person'. We seem to encounter here an unfortunate combination: a zealously religious king and a sycophantic minister willing to exploit his master's beliefs for selfish ends.
33  *Ibid.*
34  *Ibid.*, 382, 386.
35  *Ibid.*, 382.
36  Immanuel Kant, *Der Streit der Fakultäten* [The Conflict of the Faculties], trans. by Mary J. Gregor (New York: Aboris Books, 1979), 10.

37  *Ibid.*, 18. Kant intentionally worded this promise so that it applied only while Frederick Wilhelm II was still alive. After this King died in 1798, Kant considered himself absolved from this oath, and felt free to publish his *Streit der Fakultäten.*

38  *Ibid.*, 22.

39  *Ibid.*

40  *Ibid.*, 24.

41  *Ibid.*, 26.

42  *Ibid.*, 50.

43  *Ibid.*, 26, 42.

44  *Ibid.*, 44.

45  *Ibid.*

46  *Ibid.*, 46.

47  *Ibid.*, 58.

48  W. H. Bruford, *Culture and Society in Classical Weimar* (Cambridge: Cambridge University Press, 1968), 44.

49  *Ibid.*, 50.

50  *Ibid.*

51  *Ibid.*, 259.

52  Wolfgang Goethe, *Wilhelm Meister's Apprenticeship*, trans. by T. Carlyle (New York: E. P. Dutton & Co., 1937), 250.

53  H. B. Garland, *Schiller* (Wesport, CN: Greenwood Press, 1976), 16.

54  *Ibid.*, 47–8.

55  *Ibid.*, 89. See also Eike Wolgast, 'Schiller und die Fürsten' [Schiller and the Princes] in *Schiller und die höfische Welt* [Schiller and the Courtly World] ed. Achim Aurnhammer et al. (Tübingen: Max Niemeyer Verlag, 1990), 11–12.

56  Friedrich Schiller, *Sämmtliche Werke*, v. 5, *Was kann eine Gute stehende Schaubühne eigentlich wirken* [What Can a Good Standing Theatre Really Do?] (Munich: Carl Hanner Verlag, 1967), 819.

57  *Ibid.*

58  *Ibid.*, 851.

59  *Ibid.*, 821.

60  *Ibid.*, 831.

61  H. B. Garland, 125.

62  Max Steinmetz, ed., *Geschichte der Universität Jena* [History of the University of Jena], vol. 1 (Jena: Veb Gustav Fischer Verlag, 1958), 267.

63  H. B. Garland, 140.

64  Steinmetz, 1:230.

65  Gerhert Schmid, 'Einleitung', in Friedrach Strack, ed., *Evolution des Geistes: Jena um 1800* [Evolution of the Mind: Jena in 1800] (Stuttgart: Klett-Cotta, 1994, 16.

66  Steinmetz, 1:176.

67  *Ibid.*, 178.

68  *Ibid.*, 177.

69  Otto Dann, 'Jena in der Epoche der Revolution', in Strack, 18.

70  *Ibid.*, 27.

71  Friedrich Schiller, *Sämmtliche Werke*, vol. 10, *Was Heisst und zu welchem Ende studiert man Universalgeschichte?* [What is and to What End Does

One Study Universal History?] (Stuttgart: J. G. Cottaschen Buchhandlung, 1887), 294.

72 *Ibid.*
73 *Ibid.*, 295.
74 *Ibid.*, 295–6.
75 *Ibid.*, 296.
76 *Ibid.*, 296.
77 H. B. Garland, 138; Steinmetz, 1:270.
78 J. G. Fichte, *Early Philosophical Writings*, trans. Daniel Breazeale (Ithaca: Cornell University Press, 1988), 15.
79 J. G. Fichte, *Sämmtliche Werke*, vol. 6, *Züruckforderung der Denkfreiheit von den Fürsten Europeans, die sie bisher unterdrückte* [Reclamation of Freedom of Thought from the Princes of Europe, Who Have Hitherto Suppressed It] (Berlin: Veit Verlag, 1845), 1.
80 Fichte, *Early Writings*, 137.
81 *Ibid.*, 152.
82 *Ibid.*
83 *Ibid.*, 169.
84 *Ibid.*, 172.
85 *Ibid.*, 176.
86 *Ibid.*, 83.
87 *Ibid.*, 105.
88 J. G. Fichte, *The Science of Knowledge (Wissenschaftslehre)*, trans. by Peter Heath and John Lacks (New York: Appleton-Century-Crofts, 1970), 4.
89 *Ibid.*, 16.
90 *Ibid.*, 97.
91 *Ibid.*, 3.
92 *Ibid.*, 19–20.
93 *Ibid.*, 20.
94 Steinmetz, 1:251.
95 *Ibid.*
96 Fichte, *Early Writings*, 84.
97 *Ibid.*, 21.
98 R. Lassahn, *Studien zur Wirkungeschichte Fichte als Pädagogue* [Studies on a Working History of Fichte as Pedagogue] (Heidelberg: Quelle & Meyer, 1970), 36.
99 Fichte, *Science of Knowledge*, 6.
100 Lassahn, 39.
101 *Ibid.*
102 *Ibid.*, 41–2.
103 Fichte, *Early Writings*, 29.
104 See Fichte's *Die Grundzüge des gegenwärtigen Zeitalters* [The Basic Features of the Present Age], published in 1806.
105 Fichte, *Early Writings*, 17.
106 Steinmetz, 1:251.
107 For a thorough discussion of Winkelmann and Lessing, see E. M. Butler, *The Tyranny of Greece Over Germany* (Boston: Beacon Press, 1958).
108 Haym, *Die romantische Schule* (Berlin: Weidmannsche Buchhandlung, 1920), 151.

109   *Ibid.*, 168.
110   *Ibid.*, 171–2.
111   *Ibid.*, 185–92.
112   *Ibid.*, 172.
113   *Ibid.*, 187. Cf. the dualistic view of man in Hamlet's great soliloquy, 'What a piece of work is a man . . .'
114   Paul Kluckhohn, *Deutsche Romantik* (Leipzig: Velhagen und Klaping, 1924), 42. Kluckhohn argues that before F. Schlegel, the term *'romantik'* referred to *'Roman'* – that is, to the novel. But Schlegel, Novalis and others of the Jena school began using the term in the new, modern sense.
115   Friedrich Schlegel, *Kritische Ausgabe*, vol. 2, *Athenäum Fragmente* (Zürich: Verlag Ferdinand Schönirgh, 1979), 182.
116   *Ibid.*, 183.
117   *Ibid.*
118   *Ibid.*
119   Friedrich Schlegel, *Über das Studium der griecheschen Poesie* [On the Study of Greek Poetry], ed. by Paul Hankamer (Godesburg: Verlag Helmut Küpper, 1947), 48.
120   Clemens Menze, *Der Bildungsbegiff des jungen Friedrich Schlegel* [The Educational Theory of the Young Friedrich Schlegel] (Ratigen: A. Henn Verlag, 1964), 8.
121   *Ibid.*, 12.
122   *Ibid.*, 8.
123   *Ibid.*, 13.
124   *Ibid.*, 14.
125   Haym, 615.
126   Heinrich Knittermeyer, *Schelling und die romantische Schule* (Munich: Verlag Ernst Reinhardt, 1929), 40.
127   Haym, 625.
128   Knittermeyer, 61.
129   Steinmetz, 1:253.
130   *Ibid.*; Haym, 655.
131   Haym, 655.
132   Haym, 656.
133   F. W. J. Schelling, *On University Studies*, trans. by E. Morgan (Athens, OH: Ohio University Press, 1966), 6.
134   Morgan, p. 9; 1803 edn, 11.
135   Morgan, 12n.
136   *Ibid.*, 6.
137   Schelling, *Über Acad. Stud.* (1803), 66.
138   *Ibid.*
139   Morgan, 27; Schelling (1803 edn), 49.
140   Schelling *Über Acad. Stud.* (1803), 55.
141   *Ibid.*, 54.

# Chapter 3

1 George Gordon, Lord Byron, *Byron's Letters and Journals*, ed. by Leslie Marchand, vol. 1 (Cambridge, MA: Harvard University Press, 1973), 208.
2 *Ibid.*, 80.
3 *Ibid.*, 78.
4 *Ibid.*, 124.
5 Ethel Colburn Mayne, *Byron* (London: Methuen & Co., Ltd., 1924), 64.
6 Byron, *Letters*, 1:148.
7 *Ibid.*, 135.
8 *Ibid.*, 80.
9 William Hazlitt, *The Complete Works of William Hazlitt*, ed. P. P. Howe, vol. 8 (New York: AMS Press, Inc., 1967) (1967), 268.
10 Kenneth Curry, *Southey* (London: Routledge & Kegan Paul, 1975), 18.
11 Newman Ivey White, *Shelley*, vol. 1 (New York: Alfred A. Knopf, 1940), 105.
12 *Ibid.*, 115.
13 *Ibid.*, 116.
14 Percy Bysshe Shelley, *The Letters of Percy Bysshe Shelley*, ed. by L. Jones (Oxford: Clarendon Press, 1964), 55.
15 *Ibid.*, 56.
16 *Ibid.*
17 Ben Ross Schneider, Jr., *Wordsworth's Cambridge Education* (Cambridge: Cambridge University Press, 1957), 4.
18 *Ibid.*, 7.
19 *Ibid.*, p. 41. Cf also William Wordsworth, *The Prelude*, ed. Jonathan Wordsworth (New York: W. W. Norton and Company, 1979), III, 44–50. (All citations to *The Prelude* are from the 1805 version and give book and line numbers.)
20 Searby, 572.
21 But Searby, in the 'Wordsworth and Cambridge's Informal Curriculum' section of his history of Cambridge, is critical of Schneider's account and argues that Wordsworth was not as alienated at Cambridge as Schneider says.
22 *Prelude* IV, 140–2.
23 Cassius Longinus(?), *De Sublimate* [On the Sublime], trans. by A. O. Prickard (Oxford: Clarendon Press, 1906), 11–12.
24 *Ibid.*, 65.
25 *Ibid.*, 66.
26 Edmund Burke, *A Philosophical Enquiry into the Origins of Our Ideas of the Sublime and the Beautiful* (London: R. & J. Dodsley, 1759), 58–60.
27 Wordsworth, *The Prelude*, VI, 452–6.
28 *Ibid.*, 520–4.
29 *Ibid.*, XIII, 451–2.
30 Schneider, ch. 4 ('Apprentice Poet').
31 William Wordsworth and Dorothy Wordsworth, *The Letters of William and Dorothy Wordsworth*, ed. by Ernest de Selincourt (Oxford: Clarendon Press, 1967), 24.
32 Schneider, ix.

33  De Quincey, *Collected Works*, ed. by David Masson, vol. 2, *Autobiography* (Edinburgh: Adam and Charles Black, 1889), 24.
34  *Ibid.*, 62.
35  M. H. Abrams and others, eds., *The Norton Anthology of English Literature*, vol. 2 (New York: W. W. Norton & Company, 1986), 462.
36  De Quincey, *Collected Works*, 2:4.
37  *Ibid.*, 10.
38  *Ibid.*, 31.
39  *Ibid.*, 32. Judging from the experiences of Schiller, Fichte and others, one can see some justification for this remark.
40  *Ibid.*
41  *Ibid.*, 41.
42  *Ibid.*, 20.
43  Samuel Coleridge, *Collected Works*, ed. R. J. White, vol. 1, *Lectures 1795 on Politics and Religion* (Princeton, NJ: Princeton University Press, 1972), 205.
44  *Ibid.*, 210.
45  *Ibid.*
46  For a short time in 1798, Coleridge served as a Unitarian preacher at Shrewsbury.
47  Samuel Coleridge, *Biographia Literaria* (London: J. M. Dent & Co., n.d.), 334.
48  J. Robert Barth, S.J., *Coleridge and Christian Doctrine* (Cambridge, MA: Harvard University Press, 1969), 168.
49  Coleridge, *Biographia Literaria*, 144.
50  Fichte, *Wissenschaftslehre*, 97.
51  Coleridge, *Biographia Literaria*, 78.
52  *Ibid.*, 144–5.
53  *Ibid.* Cf. Acts 17:28.
54  David P. Calleo, *Coleridge and the Idea of the Modern State* (New Haven, CT: Yale University Press, 1981), 82.
55  *Ibid.*, 83.
56  Coleridge, *Collected Works*, 1:6.
57  Samuel Coleridge, *Collected Works*, ed. by R. J. White, vol. 6, *Lay Sermons* (Princeton, NJ: Princeton University Press, 1972), 176.
58  *Ibid.*, 33–4.
59  *Ibid.*, 49.
60  *Ibid.*, 50.
61  *Ibid.*, 126.
62  *Ibid.*, 170.
63  Coleridge, *Collected Works*, 1:229.
64  *Ibid.*, 43.
65  Immanuel Kant, *Kant on History*, ed. Lewis White Beck (Indianapolis: Bobbs-Merrill Publishing Co. Inc., 1950), 4.
66  Coleridge, *Collected Works*, 6:229.
67  Coleridge, *Collected Works*, 1:43.
68  Coleridge, *Collected Works*, 6:40.
69  *Ibid.*, 170.
70  *Ibid.*, 186.

71 *Ibid.*, 187.
72 *Ibid.*, 40.
73 *Ibid.*, 18.
74 Samuel Coleridge, *On The Constitution of Church and State* (London: J. D. Dent & Sons Ltd, 1972), 5.
75 *Ibid.*, 4.
76 *Ibid.*, 6.
77 *Ibid.*, 33–4.
78 *Ibid.*, 33.
79 *Ibid.*, 37.

## Chapter 4

1 Heinrich Steffens, *German University Life*, trans. by William L. Gage (Philadelphia: J. B. Lippincott and Co., 1874), 179.
2 *Ibid.*, 182.
3 Schelsky, 43.
4 Max Lenz, *Geschichte der Universität Berlin* [History of the University of Berlin], vol. 1 (Halle: Verlag der Buchhandlung des Waisenhauses, 1910), 33.
5 *Ibid.*, 34.
6 *Ibid.*
7 Schelsky, 44.
8 *Ibid.*
9 Lenz, 1:72.
10 *Ibid.*, 77.
11 *Ibid.*, 26.
12 *Ibid.*, 87.
13 Schelsky, 45.
14 Lenz, 1:74.
15 *Ibid.*, 91.
16 J. G. Fichte, *Sämmtliche Werke*, vol. 8, *Deducierter Plan einer zu Berlin zu errichtenden hoheren Lehranstalt* [Deduced Plan for an Institution of Higher Learning to be Established in Berlin] (Berlin: Veit Verlag, 1846), 97.
17 Schelsky, 43.
18 Turnball, 9.
19 Schelsky, 43.
20 *Ibid.*
21 J. G. Fichte, *Fichtes Nachgelassene Werke*, vol. 3, *Ideen für die innere Organisation der Universität Erlangen* [Ideas for the Inner Organization of the University of Erlangen] (Bonn: Adolph Marcus, 1835), 275.
22 *Ibid.*, 277.
23 *Ibid.*, 278.
24 *Ibid.*, 281.
25 *Ibid.*, 291.
26 *Ibid.*, 293.
27 *Ibid.*, 294.
28 *Ibid.*, 282.

29   *Ibid.*, 283.
30   *Ibid.*, 284.
31   *Ibid.*
32   Fichte, *Sämmtliche Werke*, 8:101–2.
33   *Ibid.*, 103.
34   *Ibid.*
35   *Ibid.*, 146.
36   *Ibid.*, 141.
37   *Ibid.*, 142.
38   *Ibid.*, 135.
39   Lenz, 1:118.
40   Fichte, 8:129.
41   *Ibid.*, 161.
42   *Ibid.*, 164–5.
43   *Ibid.*
44   *Ibid.*, 170.
45   *Ibid.*, 171.
46   *Ibid.*, 174–76.
47   *Ibid.*
48   *Ibid.*, 123.
49   *Ibid.*, 113.
50   *Ibid.*, 157–8.
51   *Ibid.*
52   Lenz, 1:111.
53   J. G. Fichte, *Reden an die deutsche Nation* [Addresses to the German Nation] (Leipzig: F. A. Brockhaus, 1871), 17.
54   *Ibid.*, 20.
55   *Ibid.*, 21.
56   *Ibid.*
57   *Ibid.*, 22.
58   *Ibid.*, 29.
59   *Ibid.*, 30.
60   *Ibid.*, 113–14.
61   *Ibid.*, 13.
62   Turnball, 57–8.
63   Schelsky, 47.
64   F. Schleiermacher, *Sämmtliche Werke*, part 3, vol. 1, *Gelegentliche Gedanken über Universitäten in deutschem Sinn* [Occasional Thoughts on Universities in the German Sense] (Berlin: G. Reimer, 1846), 627.
65   *Ibid.*, 628.
66   *Ibid.*, 546.
67   *Ibid.*, 558.
68   F. Schleiermacher, *Sämmtliche Werke*, part 3, vol. 8 (Berlin: G. Reimer, 1846), 543.
69   Schleiermacher, 3:8:555.
70   *Ibid.*, 643.
71   *Ibid.*, 638.
72   Schelsky, 51.
73   Edward Spranger, *Wilhelm von Humboldt und die Reform des Bildungswesens*

[Wilhelm von Humboldt and the Reform of Education] (Berlin: Reuther und Reichard, 1910), 32–3.

74 Guy Stanton Ford, *Stein and the Era of Reform in Prussia* (Princeton, NJ: Princeton University Press, 1922), 122.

75 Lenz, 1:155.

76 *Ibid.*, 168.

77 *Ibid.*, 156.

78 *Ibid.*, 156.

79 *Ibid.*, 171.

80 Schelsky, p. 64.

81 Wilhelm von Humboldt, *Gesammelte Schriften*, vol. 1, *Theorie der Bildung des Menschen* [Theory of the Education of Man] (Berlin: B. Behr's Verlag, 1903), 285.

82 Spranger, 61.

83 *Ibid.*, 51.

84 Lenz, 1:170.

85 *Ibid.*

86 *Ibid.*, 158.

87 *Ibid.*, 169.

88 *Ibid.*, 171–2.

89 *Ibid.*, 207.

90 Wilhelm von Humboldt, *Gessamelte Schriften*, vol. 10, *Über die innere und äussere Organisation der höheren wissenschaftlichen Anstalten in Berlin* [On the Inner and Outer Organization of Higher Scientific Institutions in Berlin] (Berlin: B. Behr's Verlag, 1903), 257.

91 Lenz, 1:194.

92 Von Humboldt, 10:251.

93 *Ibid.*

94 *Ibid.* 'Einsamkeit und Freiheit'.

95 *Ibid.*, 253.

96 Schelsky, 68.

## Chapter 5

1 Stephen Prickett, *Romanticism and Religion*, 4.

2 For a good discussion of such societies, see Sheldon Rothblatt, 'The Student Sub-culture and the Examination System in Early Nineteenth Century Oxbridge', in *The University in Society*, vol. I, ed. Lawrence Stone (Princeton, NJ: Princeton University Press, 1974), 247–303.

3 Quoted in Peter Allen, *The Cambridge Apostles: The Early Years* (Cambridge: Cambridge University Press, 1978), 4.

4 *Ibid.*, 6.

5 Quoted in Allen, 141.

6 *Ibid.*, 13–14.

7 Quoted in Stephen Prickett, *Romanticism and Religion: The Tradition of Coleridge and Wordsworth* (Cambridge: Cambridge University Press, 1976), 34.

8 Quoted in Allen, 164.

9   Quoted in Charles Sanders, *Coleridge and the Broad Church Movement* (New York: Russell and Russell, 1942), 186.

10  [F. D. Maurice], 'The Universities of Europe and America – Cambridge No. II', *Athenaeum*, 17 December 1828, 943.

11  [F. D. Maurice], 'The Universities of Europe and America – Cambridge, No. I', *Athenaeum*, 8 December 1828, 911.

12  *Ibid.*

13  *Ibid.*

14  Trinity College Mss., Add. ms. a. 77[139] (2 November 1844).

15  Trinity College Mss., Add.ms.a.77[127] (13 May 1822).

16  Trinity College Mss., Add.ms.a.77[151] (17 June 1845).

17  Trinity College Mss., Add.ms.a.77[131] (30 December 1841).

18  Trinity College Mss., Add.ms.a.77[127] (13 May 1822).

19  Trinity College Mss., Add.ms.a.206[171].

20  Trinity College Mss., Add.ms.a.77[131] (30 December 1841).

21  Trinity College Mss., Add.ms.a.206[180] (20 March 1843).

22  Trinity College Mss., Add.ms.a.77[128].

23  Trinity College Mss., Add.ms.a.77[131] (30 December 1841).

24  Trinity College Mss., Add.ms.a.77[162] (15 February 1844).

25  Trinity College Mss., Add.ms.a.77[131] (30 December 1841).

26  Whewell's work in the philosophy of science has been of particular interest to recent historicans and philosophers; see Menachem Fisch, *William Whewell: Philosopher of Science* (Oxford: Clarendon Press, 1991) and Fisch and Schaeffer, eds., *William Whewell: A Composite Portrait* (Oxford: Clarendon Press, 1991) for insightful readings of his work in this area.

27  Trinity College Mss., Add.ms.c.57[1] (25 July 1825).

28  Trinity College Mss., Add.ms.a.215[19] (15 August 1827).

29  Trinity College Mss., Add.ms.c.91[107].

30  Trinity College Mss., Add.ms.c.91[108].

31  Garland, p. 88, n. 109.

32  On the Tennyson bust, see T. S. R. Montegle's letters to Whewell in Trinity College Mss., Add.ms.a.65[37, 40, 44].

33  Whewell, *Remarks* (1834), p. 22.

34  Garland, 77.

35  Whewell, 'Remarks on Some Parts of Mr. Thirlwall's Letter on the Admission of Dissenters to Academical Degrees', in *Cambridge Pamphlets*, vol. xxiii, 98.c.80.25[9], 4.

36  Charles Lyell, *Travels in America*, vol. 1 (New York: Wiley and Putnam, 1845), 247.

37  William Whewell, *The Philosophy of the Inductive Science Founded Upon their History* (London: J. W. Parker, 1847; reprint, New York: Johnson Reprint Corp., 1966), 3.

38  William Whewell, *Of a Liberal Education in General* (London: John W. Parker, 1850), 8.

39  *Grace Book O*, 1850, flyleaf.

40  *Ibid.*

41  *Report of H.M. Royal Commissioners Appointed to Inquire into the State, Discipline, Studies, and revenues of the University and Colleges of Cam-*

*bridge*, in *State Papers*, vol. LXIV, 1852, pt. 2, 'Correspondence and Evidence', p. 415.

42  *Ibid.*, pt. 1, 203.
43  *Ibid.*, 202.
44  Janet Stair Douglas, *Life of Whewell*, 392–4.
45  William Whewell, 'Considerations on the General Principals in Regard to Colleges Proposed for Consideration by the Cambridge University Commissioners', in *Trinity College Pamphlets*, Adv.c.15.57[22], 1 January 1858.
46  William Whewell, 'Suggestions Respectfully Offered to the Cambridge University Commissioners', in *Trinity College Pamphlets*, Adv.c.15.57[23], 18 January 1858.
47  *Ibid.*, 12.
48  *Ibid.*, 18.
49  *Ibid.*, 5–6.
50  Whewell, 'Consideration', 1 January 1858, 2.
51  Whewell, 'Suggestions', 1–2.
52  *Ibid.*, 3.
53  Stair Douglas, 399.
54  William Whewell, 'Remarks', 17–18.
55  *Ibid.*, 17.
56  A. Dwight Culler, *The Imperial Intellect*, 35.
57  Daniel Newsome, *The Parting of Friends*, 73.
58  Culler, 36.
59  *Ibid.*; Newsome, *Parting*, 78.
60  Newsome, *Parting*, 70.
61  Stephen Prickett, *Romanticism and Religion*, 92.
62  *Ibid.*, 93, 103.
63  *Ibid.*, 103.
64  *Ibid.*, 102.
65  Geoffrey Faber, *Oxford Apostles*, 159.
66  Culler, 54.
67  *Ibid.*, 68.
68  Meriol Trevor, *Newman*, vol. 1, 147–8.
69  *Ibid.*, 221.
70  Faber, 129.
71  *Ibid.*, 139.
72  Trevor, 224–5.
73  Matthew Arnold, *Higher Schools and Universities in Germany*, 166.
74  E. B. Pusey, *Collegiate and Professorial Teaching and Discipline*, 6–7.
75  *Ibid.*, 16–18.
76  *Ibid.*, 9–10.
77  *Ibid.*, 10.
78  *Ibid.*, 57.
79  *Ibid.*, 40.
80  *Ibid.*, 49.
81  *Ibid.*, 208.
82  *Ibid.*, 48.
83  *Ibid.*, 215.

84  *Ibid.*, 212.
85  Trevor, 285.
86  Trevor, 281–5.
87  Owen Chadwick, *Newman*, 28.
88  Newman, *Idea*, ix.
89  *Ibid.*, xiii.
90  *Ibid.*, 101.
91  *Ibid.*, 153, 162.
92  *Ibid.*, 167.
93  *Ibid.*, 120.
94  *Ibid.*, 83–91.
95  Chadwick, *Newman*, 28.
96  *Ibid.*, 51.
97  *Ibid.*, 67.
98  Newman, *Idea*, 144–5.
99  *Ibid.*, 147.
100  Newman, *Historical Sketchs*, 182.
101  Newsome, *Godliness and Good Learning*, 14.
102  Newman, *Historical Sketches*, 182.
103  *Ibid.*, 228; cf Tillyard, 95.

## Epilogue

1  Fritz Ringer, *The Decline of the German Mandarins* (Cambridge, MA: Harvard University Press, 1969), 26.
2  Max Steinmetz, ed., *Geschichte der Universität Jena* [History of the University of Jena] (Jena: Veb Gustav Fischer Verlag, 1958).
3  Trinity College MSS., Add. Ms. c.91[107], 14 May [1834].
4  Alan D. Gilbert, *The Making of post-Christian Britain* (London: Longman, 1980).

# Bibliography

Abrams, M. H. *The Mirror and the Lamp*. New York: Oxford University Press, 1953.

Abrams, M. H. and others, eds. *The Norton Anthology of English Literature*. Vol. 2. New York: W. W. Norton & Company, 1986.

Allen, Peter. *The Cambridge Apostles: The Early Years*. Cambridge: Cambridge University Press, 1978.

Arnold, Matthew. *Higher Schools and Universities in Germany*. London: Macmillan and Co., 1874.

Barth, J. Robert, S. J. *Coleridge and Christian Doctrine*. Cambridge, MA: Harvard University Press, 1969.

Barzun, Jacques. *Romanticism and the Modern Ego*. Boston: Little, Brown, and Company, 1944.

Bentham, Jeremy. *The Works of Jeremy Bentham*. Edited by John Bowring. Vol. 10. Edinburgh: William Tait, 1843.

Body, Alfred H. *John Wesley and Education*. London: The Epworth Press, 1936.

Bollnow, Otto F. *Die Pädagogik der deutschen Romantik* [German Romantic Pedagogy]. Stuttgart: W. Kohlhammer Verlag, 1952.

Boswell, James. *The Life of Samuel Johnson*. Vol. 1. London: John Murray, 1844.

Boulger, James D. *Coleridge as Religious Thinker*. New Haven, CT: Yale University Press, 1961.

Bruford, W. H. *Germany in the Eighteenth Century: The Social Background of the Literary Revival*. Cambridge: Cambridge University Press, 1968.

—— *Culture and Society in Classical Weimar*. Cambridge: Cambridge University Press, 1962.

Burke, Edmund. *A Philosophical Enquiry Into the Origins of Our Ideas of the Sublime and the Beautiful*. London: R. & J. Dodsley, 1759.

Butler, E. M. *The Tyranny of Greece over Germany*. Boston: Beacon Press, 1958.

Byron, George Gordon, Lord. *Byron's Letters and Journals*. Edited by Leslie Marchand. Vol. 1, *1798–1810*. Cambridge, MA: Harvard University Press, 1973.

Byron, George Gordon. *Poetical Works*. London: Oxford University Press, 1967.

Calleo, David P. *Coleridge and the Idea of the Modern State*. New Haven, CT: Yale University Press, 1966.

Carnall, Geoffrey. *Robert Southey and His Age*. Oxford: Clarendon Press, 1960.

Cassirer, Ernst. *Kant's Life and Thought*. Translated by James Hader. New Haven: Yale University Press, 1981.

Chadwick, Owen. *Newman*. Oxford: Oxford University Press, 1983.

Charpentier, John. *Coleridge: The Sublime Somnambulist*. Translated by M. V. Nugent. New York: Dodd, Mead, & Co., 1929.

Coleridge, Samuel Taylor. *Biographia Literaria*. London: J. M. Dent & Co., n.d.

—— *Collected Works.* Edited by R. J. White. Vol. 1, *Lectures, 1795, on Politics and Religion.* Princeton, NJ: Princeton University Press, 1972.

—— *Collected Works.* Edited by Barbara E. Rooke. Vol. 4, *The Friend.* Princeton, NJ: Princeton University Press, 1969.

—— *Collected Works.* Edited by R. J. White. Vol. 6, *Lay Sermons.* Princeton, NJ: Princeton University Press, 1972.

—— *On the Constitution of Church and State.* London: J. M. Dent & Sons Ltd, 1972.

—— *Poetical Works.* London: Macmillan & Co. Ltd, 1905.

Colmer, John. *Coleridge Critic of Society.* Oxford: Clarendon Press, 1959.

Copleston, Edward. *A Reply to the Calumnies of the Edinburgh Review Against Oxford.* Oxford: Cooke, Parker, and Mackinlay, 1810.

Copleston, Frederick, S. J. *A History of Philosophy.* Vol. 6, *Wolff to Kant.* Westminster, MD: The Newman Press, 1960.

—— *A History of Philosophy.* Vol. 7, *Fichte to Nietzsche.* Westminster, MD: The Newman Press, 1960.

Culler, Dwight A. *The Imperial Intellect.* New Haven, CT: Yale University Press, 1955.

Curry, Kenneth. *Southey.* London: Routledge & Kegan Paul, 1975.

De Quincey, Thomas. *Collected Works.* Edited by David Masson. Vol. 3, *Confessions of an English Opium Eater.* Edinburgh: Adam and Charles Black, 1890.

—— *Collected Works.* Edited by David Masson. Vol. 2, *Autobiography.* Edinburgh: Adam and Charles Black, 1889.

Duproix, Paul. *Kant et Fichte et le Problème de l'Education.* [Kant and Fichte and the Problem of Education]. Paris: Ancienne Librairie Germer Baillière, 1897.

Ellis, Amanda. *Rebels and Conservatives.* Bloomington, IN: University of Indiana Press, 1967.

Erdman, Karl Dietrick. *Kant und Schiller als Zeitgenossen der französichen Revolution.* [Kant and Schiller as Contemporaries of the French Revolution]. London: Institute of Germanic Studies, 1986.

Everett, Charles Warren. *The Education of Jeremy Bentham.* New York: Columbia University Press, 1931.

Faber, Geoffrey. *Oxford Apostles.* London: Faber and Faber, 1933.

Fichte, Johann Gottlieb. *Die Bestimmung des Menschen* [The Vocation of Man]. Hamburg: Felix Meiner, 1954.

Fichte, Johann Gottlieb. *Early Philosophical Writings.* Translated and edited by Daniel Breazeale. Ithaca, NY: Cornell University Press, 1988.

—— *Fichtes Nachgelassene Werke.* Vol. 3, *Ideen für die innere Organisation der Universität Erlangen* [Ideas for the Inner Organization for the University of Erlangen]. Bonn: Adolph Marcus, 1835.

—— *Reden an die deutsche Nation* [Addresses to the German Nation]. Leipzig: F. A. Brockhaus, 1871.

—— *Sämmtliche Werke.* Vol. 6, *Züruckforderung der Denkfreiheit von den Fürsten Europeans, die sie bisher unterdrückte* [Reclamation of Freedom of Thought from the Princes of Europe, Who Have Hitherto Suppressed It]. Berlin: Veit Verlag, 1845.

—— *Sämmtliche Werke.* Vol. 8, *Deducirter Plan einer zu Berlin zu errichtenden höheren Lehranstalt* [Deduced Plan for an Institution of Higher Learning to be Established in Berlin]. Berlin: Veit Verlag, 1846.

—— *The Vocation of Man.* Translated by William Smith and Roderik M. Chisholm. New York: The Liberal Arts Press, 1956.

—— *Science of Knowledge (Wissenschaftslehre).* Translated and edited by Peter Heath and John Lachs. New York: Appleton-Century-Crofts, 1970.

Ford, Guy Stanton. *Stein and the Era of Reform in Prussia.* Princeton, NJ: Princeton University Press, 1922.

Friedman, Michael A. *The Making of a Tory Humanist.* New York: Columbia University Press, 1979.

Garland, H. B. *Schiller.* Wesport, CN: Greenwood Press, 1976.

Garland, Martha McMackin. *Cambridge before Darwin.* Cambridge: Cambridge University Press, 1980.

Gascoigne, John. *Cambridge in the Age of the Enlightenment.* Cambridge: Cambridge University Press, 1989.

Gibbon, Edward. *Autobiographies.* Edited by John Murray. London: John Murray, 1896.

Goethe, Wolfgang. *Wilhelm Meister's Apprenticeship.* Translated by Thomas Carlyle. New York: E. P. Dutton & Co., Inc., 1937.

Gooch, G. P. *Germany and the French Revolution.* London: Frank Cass & Co. Ltd, 1965.

Haney, John Louis. *The German Influence on S. T. Coleridge.* New York: Haskell House Publishers, 1975.

Harper, George McLean. *William Wordsworth: His Life, Work, and Influence.* New York: Charles Scribner's Sons, 1923.

Haym, Rudolf. *Die Romantische Schule* [The Romantic School]. Berlin: Weidmannsche Buchhandlung, 1920.

Humboldt, Wilhelm von. *Gesammelte Schriften.* Vol. 1, *Theorie der Bildung des Menschen* [Theory of the Education of Man]. Berlin: B. Behr's Verlag, 1903.

—— *Gesammelte Schriften.* Vol. 10. *Über die innere und äussere Organisation der höheren wissenschaftlichen Anstalten in Berlin* [On the Inner and Outer Organization of Higher Scientific Institutions in Berlin]. Berlin: B. Behr's Verlag, 1903.

Kant, Immanuel. *The Critique of Judgement.* Translated by James Creed Meredith. Oxford: Clarendon Press, 1952.

—— *The Critique of Pure Reason.* Translated by Norman Kemp Smith. New York: The Modern Library, 1958.

—— *Fundamental Principles of the Metaphysics of Morals.* Translated by Thomas K. Abbot. Indianapolis: Bobbs-Merrill Co. Inc., 1949.

—— *Observations on the Feeling of the Beautiful and Sublime.* Translated by John T. Goldthwait. Berkeley: University of California Press, 1960.

Kant, Immanuel. *On History.* Edited and translated by Lewis White Beck. Indianapolis: Bobbs-Merrill Company, Inc., 1963.

—— *Prolegomena to Any Future Metaphysics.* Edited by Lewis White Beck. Indianapolis: Bobbs-Merrill Publishing Co. Inc., 1950.

—— *Der Streit der Fakultäten* [The Conflict of the Faculties]. Translated by Mary J. Gregor. New York: Aboris Books, 1979.

—— *Werke.* Edited by Wilhelm Weischedel. Vol. 11, *Beantwortung der Frage:*

*Was ist Aufklärung* [Answer to the Question: What is Enlightenment?].
Frankfurt: Surhkamp Verlag, 1964.
—— *Werke*. Edited by Wilhelm Weischedel. Vol. 12, *Über Pädagogik* [On
Pedagogy]. Frankfurt: Insel Verlag, 1964.
Ker, Ian. *John Henry Newman: A Biography*. Oxford: Clarendon Press, 1988.
Kluckhohn, Paul. *Die deutsche Romantik* [German Romanticism]. Leipzig:
Velhagen und Klaping, 1924.
Knittermeyer, Heinrich. *Schelling und die romantische Schule* [Schelling and
the Romantic School]. Munich: Verlag Ernst Reinhardt, 1929.
Knox, Vicesimus. *Liberal Education: or, a Practical Treatise on the Methods of
Acquiring Useful and Polite Learning*. London: Charles Dilly, 1788.
Krieger, Leonard. *The German Idea of Freedom*. Boston: Beacon Press, 1957.
Lassahn, Rudolf. *Studien zur Wirkungeschichte Fichtes als Pädagoge* [Studies
on a Working History of Fichte as Pedagogue]. Heidelberg: Quelle & Meyer,
1970.
Lenz, Max. *Geschichte der Universität Berlin* [History of the University of
Berlin]. Vol. 1. Halle: Verlag der Buchhandlung des Waisenhauses, 1910.
Lessing, Gotthold Ephraim. *Werke*. Vol. 8, *Die Erziehung des Menschengeschlechts*
[The Education of the Human Race]. Munich: Carl Hanser Verlag, 1979.
Longinus, Cassius[?]. *On the Sublime*. Translated by A. O. Prickard. Oxford:
Clarendon Press, 1906.
Luards, Henry Richards. *Graudati Cantabrigienses* [Graduates of Cambridge].
Cambridge: Cambridge University Press, 1884.
Lyell, Charles. *Travels in America*. Vol. 1. New York: Wiley and Putnam,
1845.
[Maurice, Frederick Denison]. 'Sketches of Contemporary Authors No. V:
Mr. Wordsworth', *Athenaeum* 8 (19 February 1828): 113–15.
[Maurice, Frederick Denison]. 'The Universities of Europe and America –
Cambridge No. I', *Athenaeum* 58 (3 December 1828): 911–12.
[Maurice, Frederick Denison]. 'The Universities of Europe and America –
Cambridge No. II', *Athenaeum* 60 (17 December 1828): 943–4.
Mayne, Ethel Colburn. *Byron*. London: Methuen & Co. Ltd, 1924.
McClelland, Charles E. *State, Society, and University in Germany, 1700–1914*.
Cambridge: Cambridge University Press, 1980.
Menze, Clemens. *Der Bildungsbegriff des jungen Friedrich Schlegel* [The Educa-
tional Theory of the Young Friedrich Schlegel]. Ratigen: A. Henn Verlag,
1964.
Michaelis, J. D. *Raisonnement über die protestantischen Universitäten in Deutschland*
[Reasonings over the Protestant Universities in Germany]. Frankfurt and
Leipzig: Privately printed, 1768.
Moorman, Mary. *William Wordsworth, a Biography*, vol. 1, *Early Years*. Ox-
ford: Clarendon Press, 1951.
Newman, John Henry, Cardinal. *Apologia Pro Vita Sua*. London: J. M. Dent
& Sons Ltd., 1955.
—— *The Idea of a University*. Westminster, MD: Christian Classics, Inc., 1973.
—— *University Sketches*. London: Montague Pickering, 1876.
Newsome, David. *Godliness and Good Learning*. London: John Murray, 1961.
Newsome, David. *The Parting of Friends*. London: John Murray, 1966.
Novalis [Friedrich Leopold von Hardenberg]. *Hymns to the Night and Other*

*Selected Writings.* Translated by Charles E. Passage. Indianapolis: Bobbs-Merrill Company, Inc., 1960.

Oxford Historical Society. *Brasnose College Register.* Oxford: Clarendon Press, 1909.

Paulsen, Friedrich. *Die Deutschen Universitäten und das Universitätstudium* [German Universities and University Study]. Berlin: 1902; reprint Hildesheim: Georg Olms Verlagsbuchhandlung, 1966.

—— *The German Universities.* Translated by Edward Delavan Perry. New York: Macmillan & Co., 1895.

—— *Immanuel Kant.* Translated by J. E. Creighton and Albert Lefebvre. New York: Charles Scribner's Sons, 1902.

Prickett, Stephen. *Romanticism and Religion: The Tradition of Coleridge and Wordsworth.* Cambridge: Cambridge University Press, 1976.

Priestley, J. B. *William Hazlitt.* London: Longmans, Green, and Co. Ltd, 1960.

Pusey, E. B. *Collegiate and Professorial Teaching and Discipline in Answer to Professor Vaughan's Strictures.* Oxford: John Henry Parker, 1854.

'Report of H.M. Royal Commissioners Appointed to Inquire into the State, Discipline, Studies, and Revenues of the University and Colleges of Cambridge'. *State Papers,* Vol. LXIX, 1852.

Rothblatt, Sheldon. 'The Idea of the Idea of a University and its Antithesis'. In *Conversazione.* Bundoora, Australia: Latrobe University, 1989.

—— *The Revolution of the Dons.* London: Faber and Faber Ltd, 1968.

—— *Tradition and Change in English Liberal Education.* London: Faber and Faber, 1976.

Rousseau, Jean Jacques. *Emile.* Translated by Barbara Foxley. Cambridge: J. M. Dent and Sons Ltd, 1966.

—— *The Social Contract.* Translated by Maurice Cranston. New York: Penguin Books, 1984.

Schelling, F. W. J. *On University Studies.* Translated by E. E. Mortan. Athens, OH: Ohio University Press, 1966.

Schelling, F. W. J. *Vorlesungen über die Methode des academischen Studium* [Lectures on the Method of Academic Study]. Tübingen: J. G. Cottaschen Verlag, 1803.

Schelsky, Helmut. *Einsamkeit und Freiheit* [Solitude and Freedom]. Düsseldorf: Bertelsmann Universitätsverlag, 1971.

Schiller, Friedrich. *Complete Works.* Translated by Charles J. Hempel, M. D. Philadelphia: I. Kohler, 1861.

—— *Sämmtliche Werke.* Vol. 5, *Wass kann eine gute stehende Schaubühne eigentlich wirken?* [What Can a Good Standing Theatre Really Do?]. Munich: Carl Hanner Verlag, 1967.

—— *Sämmtliche Werke.* Vol. 10, *Was heisst und zu welchem Ende studiert man Universalgeschichte?* [What is and to What End Does One Study Universal History?]. Stuttgart: J. G. Cottaschen Buchhandlung, 1887.

—— *Sämmtliche Werke.* Vol. 12, *Ueber das Erhabene* [On the Sublime]. Stuttgart: J. G. Cottaschen Buchhandlung, 1887.

—— *Über die ästhetische Erziehung des Menschen* [On the Aesthetic Education of Man]. Edited by Wolfgang Düsing. Munich: Carl Hanser Verlag, 1981.

Schlegel, Friedrich. *Über das Studium der griechischen Poesie* [On the Study of

Greek Poetry]. Edited by Paul Hankamer. Godesburg: Verlag Helmut Küpper, 1947.

Schleiermacher, Friedrich. *Sämmtliche Werke*. Part 3, Vol. 1, *Gelegentliche Gedanken über Universitäten in deutschem Sinn* [Occasional Thoughts on Universities in the German Sense]. Berlin: G. Reimer, 1846.

Schneider, Ben Ross, Jr. *Wordsworth's Cambridge Education*. Cambridge: Cambridge University Press, 1957.

Sedgwick, Adam. *A Discourse on the Studies of the University*. Cambridge: Pitt Press, 1833; reprint, New York: Humanities Press, 1969.

Searby, Peter. *A History of Cambridge University*. Vol. 3, *1750–1870*. Cambridge: Cambridge University Press, 1997.

Sheehan, James. *German History, 1770–1866*. Oxford: Clarendon Press, 1989.

Shelley, Percy Bysshe. *The Letters of Percy Bysshe Shelley*. Edited by Frederick L. Jones. Oxford: Clarendon Press, 1964.

Smith, Adam. *An Inquiry into the Nature and Causes of the Wealth of Nations*. New York: The Modern Library, 1937.

Southey, Robert. *The Life of Wesley*. New York: Harper and Brothers, 1847.

Schmidt, Siegfried and others, eds. *Alma Mater Jenensis*. Weimar: Hermann Böhlaus Nachfolger, 1983.

Spranger, Edward. *Wilhelm von Humboldt und die Reform des Bildungswesens* [Wilhelm von Humboldt and the Reform of Education]. Berlin: Reuther und Reichard, 1910.

Stair Douglas, Janet. *The Life and Selections from the Correspondence of William Whewell*. London: C. Kegan Paul & Co., 1881.

Steffens, Heinrich. *German University Life*. Translated by William L. Gage. Philadelphia: J. B. Lippincott and Co., 1874.

Steinmetz, Max, ed. *Geschichte der Universität Jena* [History of the University of Jena]. Vols. 1 and 2. Jena: Veb Gustav Fischer Verlag, 1958.

Strack, Friedrich, ed. *Evolution des Geistes: Jena um 1800* [Evolution of the Spirit: Jena around 1800]. Stuttgart: Klett-Cotta, 1994.

Strack, Friedrich, and others, eds. *Schiller und die höfische Welt* [Schiller and the Courtly World]. Tübingen: Max Niemeyer Verlag, 1990.

Sutherland, L. S. and L. G. Mitchell, eds. *The History of the University of Oxford*. Vol. V, *The Eighteenth Century*. Oxford: Clarendon Press, 1986.

Tillyard, A. I. *A History of University Reform*. Cambridge: W. Heffer and Sons Ltd, 1913.

Trevor, Meriol. *Newman*. Vol. 1, *The Pillar of Cloud*. London: Macmillan and Co. Ltd, 1962.

Turnball, G. H. *The Educational Theory of G. H. Fichte*. London: The University Press of Liverpool Ltd, 1926.

Vorländer, Karl. *Kant–Schiller–Goethe*. Leipzig: Felix Meier Verlag, 1923.

Walzel, Oskar. *German Romanticism*. Translated by Alma Elise Lusskey. New York: G. P. Putnam's Sons, 1932.

Ward, W. R. *Georgian Oxford*. Oxford: Clarendon Press, 1958.

Whewell, William. *Of a Liberal Education in General*. London: John W. Parker, 1850.

—— *The Philosophy of the Inductive Science Founded Upon Their History* London: John W., Parker, 1847; reprint, New York: Johnson Reprint Corp., 1966.

White, Newman Ivey. *Shelley.* Vol. 1. New York: Alfred A. Knopf, 1940.

Winstanley, D. A. *Early Victorian Cambridge.* Cambridge: Cambridge University Press, 1940.

—— *Unreformed Cambridge.* Cambridge: Cambridge University Press, 1935.

Wordsworth, Christopher. *Social Life at the English Universities in the Eighteenth Century.* Cambridge: Deighton, Bell, and Co., 1874.

Wordsworth, Dorothy. *Journals of Dorothy Wordsworth.* Edited by Mary Moorman. Oxford: Oxford University Press, 1971.

Wordsworth, William. *The Prelude.* Edited by Jonathan Wordsworth. New York: W. W. Norton and Company, 1979.

Wordsworth, William and Dorothy Wordsworth. *The Letters of William and Dorothy Wordsworth.* Edited by Ernest de Selicourt. Oxford: Clarendon Press, 1967.

Zeeden, Leonard. *Die Entstehung der Konfessionen* [The Rise of Confessions]. Munich: R. Oldenbourg, 1964.

# Index